DELIGHT
KINGDOM IDENTITY & INHERITANCE

BY
STEVE HAWKINS

Kingdom Publishers

Copyright© Steve Hawkins 2025

All rights reserved. No part of this book may be reproduced in any form by photocopying or any electronic or mechanical means, including information storage or retrieval systems, without permission in writing from both the copyright owner and the publisher of the book. The right of Steve Hawkins to be identified as the author of this work has been asserted by him in accordance with the Copyright, Designs, and Patents Act 1988 and any subsequent amendments thereto.

A catalogue record for this book is available from the British Library.

All Scripture quotations and references have been taken from the New American Standard version of the Bible and Lockman Foundation (www.Lockman.org)

ISBN: 978-1-916801-26-4

1st Edition 2025 by Kingdom Publishers, London, UK.

You can purchase copies of this book from any leading bookstore or at:

www.kingdompublishers.co.uk

Contents

INTRODUCTION	7
1 THE CROSS IS STILL THE CRUX	13
2 IDENTITY IS KEY	21
3 ALL DEBT PAID	29
4 MISSION POSSIBLE	37
5 RULERS SIT	49
6 ON EARTH, AS IT IS IN HEAVEN	57
7 HEAVEN – GLORIOUS DESTINATION AND OUR BASE NOW	63
8 THE LAMB'S BOOK OF LIFE	77
9 AMBASSADORS	83
10 BLOOD – UNDERSTOOD IN HEAVENLY PLACES	89
11 MOTIVES	97
12 FIVE REASONS TO YIELD	105
13 DAILY REST	115
14 WAG THE DOG – WHOSE GLORY?	123
15 NOISE	129
16 LIVES OF WORSHIP	139
17 LONE RANGERS	145
18 HOW MANY CHURCHES?	151
19 THE POWER OF THE TONGUE	156
20 WINEMAKER	163
POSTSCRIPT LITTLE OLD LADY	171
NOTES	177
ABOUT THE AUTHOR	179

INTRODUCTION

As the Trinity gleefully created the heavens and the earth, we read that the Holy Spirit *danced*. I understand that the literal meaning for "rejoiced" or similar, according to many of our translations of the verse in Proverbs 8, is "twirled."

How many believers have this notion of the Spirit of God as a reality in their lives? It was a delicious surprise to me, for sure.

But that's right — we read of the Three-in-One taking rapturous delight in their workmanship, the project culminating in the bringing forth of the "sons of men."

> " 26 While He had not yet made the earth and the [l]fields, Nor the first dust of the world. 27 When He established the heavens, I was there, When He inscribed a circle on the face of the deep, 28 When He made firm the skies above, When the springs of the deep became [l]fixed, 29 When He set for the sea its boundary So that the water would not transgress His [k]command, When He marked out the foundations of the earth; 30 Then I was beside Him, *as* a master workman; And I was daily *His* delight, [l]Rejoicing always before Him, 31 [m]Rejoicing in the world, His earth, And *having* my delight in the sons of men."
> PROVERBS 8: 26-31

The Trinity still delights in us. And, many are discovering and experiencing this delight, perhaps to degrees previously unimagined.

It is God's plan that we should know who we truly are, as people of Heaven, that our identity in Jesus Christ should be rock solid. Our enjoyment of our faith walk and our effectiveness in His Kingdom adventures are tied to this intrinsic appreciation of what it means to be a son of the House. There are, and there will be, plenty of media messages making a concerted effort to inform us otherwise. Their aim is to keep us very much earth-bound. But God says:

> "Therefore, if you have been raised up with Christ, keep seeking the things above, where Christ is, seated at the right hand of God. ² [a]Set your mind on the things above, not on the things that are on earth. ³ For you have died and your life is hidden with Christ in God.
>
> ⁴ When Christ, who is our life, is revealed, then you also will be revealed with Him in glory."
> COLOSSIANS 3: 1-4

God's plan in Jesus Christ is very much on track and advancing, and we are very much part of it. Father, Son and Holy Spirit are passionately pursuing their delightful purpose of revealing the Kingdom of Heaven to, and through, His Church.

Religion is giving way to revelation. Tired traditions that have perhaps sapped our energies rather than transmitted the Life of God are making way for His truth. The whole Bible is the living, breathing word of God and carries the heartbeat of the Father.

God is love, and there is no darkness at all in Him. He is pure, pulsating, alive, delightful and compassionate. He is for us. He is rooting for us. He is very much involved in all that pertains to us, His treasured investments.

Christians are discovering the delight of their true identities and realising the power of the Cross in their life experiences. The purpose of this book is to encourage you to intentionally live more deeply and more securely in yours. You are going to wake up, rub your sore eyes and begin to see life colours that, perhaps, you never knew existed. Or maybe you didn't think you were quite qualified.

Rest assured that he who writes these words has walked with the Saviour for some forty years. Yes, I've walked, triumphed, stumbled, fallen, wept, experienced rescue and compassion and the holding arms of Jesus. He has been more faithful than I could even begin to describe, though I will probably need to have a go at articulating His nature and His unwavering generosity.

He has shown me that I count; it is preposterous and yet glorious, to me, that the Lord cares enough to have shown me that His abundant life has nothing to do with deadening, legalistic religion. I am so grateful. I find myself vocalizing my gratitude ever increasingly.

Does the Church need evangelists as mouthpieces to the world around us? Of course. Does the Church also need to listen to its own evangelists? Absolutely. It is time for the sons and daughters of the Kingdom to be revealed. It is time for us all in the Body to wake up to our identity and to our inheritance, because 'getting saved' is really just the beginning. It is awesome – but it is the beginning of a unique, divine journey that carries heavenly mandates.

Many believers are in cages; prisons of religion, regret and wrong roles. Some have struggled to settle, like jigsaw pieces jammed into places that do not truly fit.

The Holy Spirit is on a dedicated mission to fix our understanding of who we are in Jesus.

> "Now the Lord is the Spirit, and where the Spirit of the Lord is, there is liberty…"
> 2 CORINTHIANS 3:17

I once heard that a sound definition of true humility is along these lines, "Knowing God as He really is and knowing who we truly are."

Such a sense of identity leaves no room for 'woe is me' gloom or 'I am so unworthy' self-deprecation; neither of those notions is remotely true as, I hope, this book will affirm. The Cross has purchased life that is far more abundant and significant than them.

This is truly a time to embrace the truth of the Gospel and its ambitions for our lives.

"When your identity is found in Christ, your identity never changes. You are always a child of God."

Tim Tebow

1
THE CROSS IS STILL THE CRUX

I previously published a book entitled, "Blood and Glory: The Cross is still the Crux." I had found the Cross (I use the capital C to designate the cross of Jesus Christ) beyond just simply relevant, or even amazing. I was so impacted by the crucial centrality of the Cross to God's design for our lives.

It was and is, unequivocally, almost unbelievably good news. If we will allow ourselves to dream beyond the ordinary, it is gloriously believable and transforms us from the inside out.

Heaven is earnestly and deeply downloading the stunning ramifications of Jesus Christ's work on the Cross to His people. Mere theology – and the theology alone is truly magnificent – is becoming upgraded to experiential, abundant life.

To be ready for what is coming upon the earth – socially, politically and spiritually - we will need to have 'hearts of flesh,' a living reality of the Cross life. Head knowledge, alone, is not going to be enough. There is a very real spiritual conflict taking place and only those who are armoured in God's spiritual equipment will be ready for these realities.

The Church is going to be gloriously and powerfully manifested; at the same time, standing for the Christian gospel is going to become ever more a challenge and society will shift further to seek to constrict Christian voices and values. Ignoring Christ, sneering at His values, and outright mockery has been and will be on the menu.

The Cross of Christ was a cosmic event that has forever changed human potential and destiny. And you, I and all believers get to walk it out. The glorious foundation is set solidly in the word of God:

> "¹² And there is salvation in no one else; for there is no other name under heaven that has been given among men by which we must be saved."
> ACTS 4:12

Saved. Saved from death. Saved from sin and its penalties. Saved from pointless, aimless living. Saved, too, from religious, deficit living.

Self-effort, striving and soulish programs have disappointed us. Never feeling good enough, judging oneself unspiritual and considering others far more qualified in their faith walk, have been the shadows accompanying many.

There is no Plan B in God's marvellous economy. The Cross has triumphed and the Church, each of us who have come to know Him, was born to demonstrate that victory.

Jesus alone is our forever companion, our confidante and our supernatural source and supply in Heaven's purposes. A religious life is one thing. A life reconciled to the Father in Heaven is totally something else.

> "⁶Jesus said to him, "I am the way, and the truth, and the life; no one comes to the Father but through Me."
> JOHN 14:6

No cross, no salvation. No salvation, no Saviour or relationship with the Father. No Saviour? Then let us eat, drink and party, as Ecclesiastes suggests in a more pessimistic moment. What would be left for us, but to try to medicate and mask our emptiness in our own, wearying strength, desperately seeking to make something of this life? And we may help a few others to do the same along the way.

Or…Hallelujah! What if our God has endowed us with something immeasurably beyond that depressing offering and hopelessly limiting prospect?

There is simply no getting around the Cross. Jesus describes Himself as the 'door' to the sheep pen and the Cross is that heavenly entrance through which the old life can be disarmed, and the new creation of Christ be born and nurtured.

Born, nurtured, matured. Brothers and sisters of this blood-bought family supporting one another in growth, in trial, in discovery.

Each Christian a vital cog in the wheel; each one uniquely fashioned by the Creator to play a colourful, fruitful part. In Jesus, we realise our heavenly design! How pointless are the world's efforts to conform behaviours, and to seek to mould people to suit others' expectations. This is not for us in the Kingdom.

We know, don't we, that someone can attend church for many years and not actually be a born-again believer. How about the countless believers who have been active for equally as many years, and yet have lived aimless, religious lives of drudgery and self-accusation? How can this possibly be the 'abundant life' that the Bible promises?

Revelation of the Cross is lethal to such a dulled and demeaning mindset. The power of the Cross deals with long-standing regrets, shame and captivating memories. At the Cross, we are relieved of the weights that may have hindered us for so long.

Surely, the Lord is the Spirit, and where He is, there is freedom and deliverance, (2 Corinthians 3:17). Not just deliverance *from* the old ways of thinking and judgements and failings, but deliverance *into* the life that Jesus has purposed for us. He is so good. He is so kind. He is on our side. And He is sure of His Kingdom purposes that He calls us to participate in.

We are going to be reminded in these following pages that Jesus' words, 'It is finished,' are a cry of victorious, liberating freedom. They apply to us today as deeply as they have ever delighted the hearts of those who have walked in Christ before us.

The Holy Spirit's heart is to enable us to function as those who have been liberated and empowered. He is not merely trying to help us to help ourselves. He is asking us to allow Him to do the transforming work. We get to take on 'an easy yoke' (Matthew 11) and, in so doing, we partner with the Kingdom power of the indwelling Spirit of God.

Our pride has to back off, right? There is no Kingdom glory for us in our own efforts. There is glory for us in Jesus as He is glorified through our lives.

> "²²The glory which You have given Me I have given to them,
> that they may be one, just as We are one;"
> JOHN 17:22

I love the testimony of Peter and Rose Eldridge at New Zion Christian Fellowship in Welwyn Garden City, UK. People have often asked these leaders just how they have managed to 'get' the church body to function so apparently seamlessly. They both just smile and say that they have no idea! They invite the Holy Spirit to lead His church – and He seems very good at it!

Churches may be very well organized and that, in itself, is not a bad thing. But has the Holy Spirit been organized *out* of Church life? If the Lord is truly leading a church, I would be surprised if consecutive meetings/services were alike. And there will be 'God incidents' scattered through the daily lives of its people.

Here we are in 2024, over two thousand years following the historical earth event called the crucifixion of Jesus of Nazareth. Yet, that event is coursing through the veins of millions of people, today, all over the world, across cultures, ethnicities, educational levels and family backgrounds.

The Cross *is* still the crux. An acceptance and aligning of one's life to the purpose and work of the Cross of Jesus *is* the key. Therein lies a relationship with the Lord, Himself; a personal life with Him and among His people.

Imagine the possibilities of how the Lord might network His people together if each one of us were secure in our identity. Because we are, and always will be, one Church. I have more to say on this, later.

Jesus went to the Cross so that we didn't have to, is that right?. We often hear this and we get the point - He took our sin and suffering upon Himself. Except – the Scripture tells us that we *did* go and were crucified with Him.

> "I have been crucified with Christ; and it is no longer I who
> live, but Christ lives in me; and the *life* which I now live in the

flesh I live by faith in the Son of God, who loved me and gave Himself up for me."
GALATIANS 2:20

We cannot crucify ourselves; we cannot deny ourselves to any degree that could accomplish such a thing as the work of the Cross. Yes, the scripture talks about denying ourselves and also about dying to ourselves. We shall come to that, too!

We have to see that we were called and chosen before the foundation of the world – and that when Jesus died, we died with Him. How many believers are 'trying to die?' With how many months and years of frustration? It doesn't work because such self-effort isn't supposed to work.

It would be like – and please forgive such a poor analogy – like me gifting you £100 and you spending the next five years trying to get that from me. All that effort. All that energy. *And no fruit of the £100 in your life.* You might even find a religious argument to keep you company – perhaps it's part of the 'learning process' to feel so stunted; perhaps the frustration is designed to humble us? No!

Rather, if you live in the reality of your new identity – as the recipient of £100 - you will demonstrate the benefits of that, by using the money! Profiting from it. Enjoying it!

When Paul talks about 'dying daily,' (1 Corinthians 15) he is referring to his decision to align his thinking with the truth of the gospel; he chooses to prefer the latter over his own thinking. He would have known all about religious self-denial as a schooled Pharisee.

Jews are required to follow not only The Ten Commandments, given in Exodus 20, but also a whole host of other laws. In Judaism they are called 'mitzvot' and there are 613 of them in the Torah! That is an extensive catalogue of rule-keeping. Respectfully, it must be exhausting to try to keep so many laws. Such introspection, such vigilance would be required. It sounds like a life of constant self-examination.

Thankfully, Jesus Christ has satisfied every requirement of the law for the born-again believer. In loving Jesus and in growing in friendship with Him, the law is satisfied. He has become our righteousness with the Father.

That is true, Kingdom identity. What a glorious gift. The Kingdom gift is given that the Kingdom will profit – and as it does so, we do, too.

"Spiritual identity means we are not what we do or what people say about us. And we are not what we have. We are the beloved daughters and sons of God."

Henri Nouwen

2
IDENTITY IS KEY

> "¹⁵No longer do I call you slaves, for the slave does not know what his master is doing; but I have called you friends, for all things that I have heard from My Father I have made known to you."
> JOHN 15:15

Many of today's Bible versions prefer to use the term 'servants' than 'slaves'. In terms of mentality and emotional experience, perhaps 'slaves' is relatively apt. The Cross has left us no deficits when it comes to our identity in Jesus Christ. There are no gaps, no unfinished measures, no missing elements.

Our reconciliation and restoration of relationship with Almighty God is complete in Heaven's eyes. Time will see this wholeness manifested in our life experience as, for some, many years of counter-Kingdom living are unknotted and released into the truth and reality of who we have become. Or, rather, of *Whose* we have become.

> "¹⁷Therefore if anyone is in Christ, [a]*he is* a new creature; the old things passed away; behold, new things have come."
> 2 CORINTHIANS 5:17

I cannot stress how vital it is for each born-again believer to be rock solid on their new identity in Jesus Christ. How life is lived will depend upon our genuine understanding and revelation of it. Whether opportunities are missed may depend on it. Whether the Christian life is lived abundantly, as designed, or religiously, will depend upon our grasp and application of our new life.

The enemy of our souls would have us believe that nothing supernatural has occurred and that we should 'do our best' to live a good, Christian life. He would settle for this if it meant that we were distanced from the truths that are key players in a new Kingdom.

We are no longer part of the old kingdom.

"⁹For this reason also, since the day we heard *of it*, we have not ceased to pray for you and to ask that you may be filled with the [ᵇ]knowledge of His will in all spiritual wisdom and understanding,¹⁰ so that you will walk in a manner worthy of the Lord, [ᶜ]to please *Him* in all respects, bearing fruit in every good work and [ᵐ]increasing in the [ᵇ]knowledge of God; ¹¹ strengthened with all power, according to [ᵉ]His glorious might, [ᶠ]for the attaining of all steadfastness and [ˢ]patience; joyously ¹² giving thanks to the Father, who has qualified us [ʰ]to share in the inheritance of the [ˢ]saints in Light.

¹³ [ⁱ]For He rescued us from the [ʲ]domain of darkness, and transferred us to the kingdom of [ᵏ]His beloved Son, ¹⁴ in whom we have redemption, the forgiveness of sins."
COLOSSIANS 1: 9-14

Drink this in.

Paul and his companions are praying earnestly – consistently – that the believers at Colossae will have Holy Spirit revelation of the work of the Cross. *In all spiritual wisdom and understanding.* It has to be a genuine, received revelation. Mental assent is not sufficient.

To 'walk in a manner worthy of the Lord' is a direct reference to living the new life in Christ. He paid such a price for us – not that we should strive to create our own religious walk, but that we should partner with the active work of the Cross. Such a walk – such an abundant life – is worthy of Him. It is worthy of His love. It is the gift of His love. His life alone is the power necessary for effective living.

PLEASING HIM

For many years I did my level best to 'please' the Lord. I don't think I am exaggerating when I say that I made myself ill in the process. I became so concerned with 'His will' that fear gained a significant stronghold in my life. The fear grew and became an almost obsessive desire to 'be right' with God. I came to see that such a mindset is in direct opposition to the purpose and finished work of the Cross.

Some may applaud such a mindset for its apparent zeal and sense of commitment. In truth, it's rather tragic when the very work of the Cross was designed to spare me such a lifestyle with its torments, self-measuring and self-accusation.

I was being robbed. I allowed myself to be robbed. If in doubt whether a blessing might be for me, I rejected it, not wanting to presume upon God's grace or the dictates (as I saw them) of His will. You could not have been any harder on me, than I was on myself.

Actually, the Kingdom of God was being robbed because of my chains. Our battles are very rarely just about our own lives. There is a bigger picture involved and there are wider purposes at stake. The Lord intervened to put a stop to my anguish and that story would probably need a book of its own!

Let us consider Jesus, in the Jordan River, about to be baptised.

Heaven opens and the Father's voice declares His delight in his son, (Matthew 3:17). He declares that He is well pleased with Him. He hasn't done anything yet.

Because - the Father's delight is an identity issue, a family issue. It isn't a slave scenario.
Colossians 1 continues to show us that as we please Him in *this* way, from a position of 'already-accepted', our lives will be *bearing fruit in every good work.*

Flowers, shrubs, trees – they bear fruit, right? They drink, they absorb sunlight. As a natural consequence, fruit is produced. The design works well and efficiently. How many of us have enjoyed the 'labour' of the Lord, in which we live *strengthened with all power according to His glorious might?*

How many of us truly understand that we have been born again into an inheritance? The saints in Light possess an inheritance. If inheritances are only received upon the death of a benefactor, how is it that we have already been qualified to share?

Well, Christ died. And we died with Him. Our eternal life has begun. If any person is in Christ, he is a new creation. The old has gone and the new has come. Life from Heaven is not only our future hope but is designed to be, to a degree, a very present reality.

A useful analogy, for me, involves football.

WHICH COLOUR SHIRT?

We have read Paul's encouragement, that Christ has *transferred* us.

As I write, the 2023-2024 football season is drawing to a close. I won't distract you with my predictions for this season's honours, except to say that my claret and blue heart is on the verge of yet another "nearly" year.

Should West Ham United rise too high in the league table, my club seems to develop a seasonal nosebleed. I consider our recent star captain – Declan Rice. A terrific, gifted midfielder, transferred to local London rivals, Arsenal, earlier in the season.

Transferred, Declan *has to* identify utterly with his new club. All previous efforts on behalf of his former employer have ceased. They are no longer applicable. He is dressed in a different colour shirt. He is dressed – may I put it this way – in new robes.

Declan's face is all over Arsenal's stadium, merchandise, and media. Of course, it is. He is no longer a man of the claret and blue – he is *their* player. He is under new management. He is training and working towards a new cause. His ambitions lie with his new club. He wants to win. He is part of a group that moves together towards shared goals, (no pun intended.) His fellowship circle has changed. The instructions he heeds have changed. His feet no longer walk in the corridors of West Ham.

Wouldn't it be odd – *wholly inappropriate* – if Declan continued to spend any of his energies on furthering the cause of a rival team, even his former club? Declan has already returned to the London Stadium, home of West Ham, with his new team, Arsenal. Imagine the fury, the outcry, if several misplaced passes during that game were identified as a sympathetic reflex towards his former employers?

It doesn't matter how many children and adults who support the Hammers, are still sporting their hard-earned replica shirts with RICE emblazoned across the back. RICE on shirts, on school equipment, on mugs, on posters and scarves. It does not matter anymore. It just isn't true anymore. *Feelings* don't come into it. He has been transferred and that's the end of the matter.

According to our verse in Colossians, we, too, have been transferred. We are not *being* transferred. Religions try to do that – to move you, change you, shift you into a new position. A new stance in life. Religions will sign up your soulish curiosity and keep you entertained and 'seeking' for days, months and years. The enemy will be quite happy to occupy you as long as it keeps you from meeting with Jesus.

Religions cannot transfer you from death to life. We have been redeemed, and this has been obtained, we are forgiven.

If we are not convinced that we are forgiven, we will limp along during our Christian journey. It's hard to run a race when hindered by a limp. When we make progress, the enemy will try to press the button of insecurity and doubt.

Oh, the masses of Christians who still live in guilt and regret. The Holy Spirit is on fire to put a stop to this, believe me! His heart longs to reveal freedom to the captives in His house.

There will be some uncomfortable, even painful, memories and experiences to be faced by some. But these spiritual 'boils' need to be lanced. The infections need to be healed. The lies need to be discredited and rejected.

Freedom calls from the other side. The freedom one might feel when unexpectedly released from a mind-torturing debt. What worry, anxiety and fear would flee with the proclamation that one is officially free of all debts!

"Your identity is not wrapped up in how right you get it or how perfect you can posture yourself. But, your identity is wrapped up in the grace of the Lord Jesus Christ."

Lecrae

3
ALL DEBT PAID

> "[19]Therefore, brethren, since we have confidence to enter the holy place by the blood of Jesus,[20] by a new and living way which He inaugurated for us through the veil, that is, His flesh ... [22] let us draw near with a [h]sincere heart in full assurance of faith, having our hearts sprinkled clean from an evil conscience ... [23] Let us hold fast the confession of our hope without wavering, for He who promised is faithful; [24] and let us consider how to stimulate one another to love and good deeds, [25] not forsaking our own assembling together, as is the habit of some, but encouraging one another; and all the more as you see the day drawing near."
> HEBREWS 10:19, 20,22-25

In full assurance. In Christ, your sins have been erased. Dissolved. Obliterated. Paid for.
This is true of your previous sins and any sin that you might commit in the future. As Joseph Prince has said, we walk under a waterfall of grace. Grace has become a constant, eternal provision for our lives.

EN GEDI

You have probably read of En Gedi in 1 Samuel. It was one of David's hideouts as he ran from Saul; south-east of Jerusalem and very close to the Dead Sea, En Gedi was a place of springs and running water.

Today the En Gedi Nature Reserve hosts 'David's Waterfall.' As it was those many years ago, En Gedi is a place of refreshment and relief. I have been there and have swum in the spring water and stood under the delightful, flowing waters of the fall.

Relief and refreshment. My visit to En Gedi occurred as our group trekked part of the scorching, Judean desert, on our way to Jericho. Was a swim ever as welcome as this one? Relief, yes, and I am so relieved that our identity issues have been settled in Heaven. In Christ, you are no longer a sinner.

To say, 'I am a sinner,' is to identify myself according to who I was, pre-Cross. I am now, as we saw in the last chapter, no longer a slave but a friend of Jesus Christ. I have understood that His blood was shed for me, on my behalf. In response, I said, 'Thank you Lord, from the bottom of my heart,' and He adopted me into the family of God, with the full rights of a son. I understood that my life was no longer my own but that He had bought me back (redeemed me) at a price. At the very highest price. The voluntary sacrifice of the Son of God. A divine transaction that took place.

It is crucial that we understand that the blood of Christ has emptied our sin account. In fact, the account has been deleted.

> "[19]... God was reconciling the world to himself in Christ, not counting people's sins against them. And he has committed to us the message of reconciliation."
> 2 CORINTHIANS 5:19

God is no longer counting our sins against us. He does not have a 'sin account' for his sons and daughters.

Paul says, in the letter to the Corinthians, that the message of reconciliation has been committed to us! How will we communicate this unless it is a living, breathing reality to us and one that we are living out? Are we not convinced? Do we still consider ourselves to be unworthy?

The whole point is that *He was, and is, worthy*. My righteousness before the Father is only in the Son *and it will only ever be there*.

YOU DIED

So what does Paul mean when he says that he 'dies daily?'

> "[31]I affirm, brethren, by the boasting in you which I have in Christ Jesus our Lord, I die daily."
> 1 CORINTHIANS 15:31

He not describing a life of self-effort and self-justification. He is talking about aligning Himself with the finished work of the Cross, where Christ died and where Paul died with Him. Every day he reckons upon (intentionally agrees with) that supernatural work – a completed work. Without it, where is the foundation upon which His faith stands? 'On Christ, the solid Rock, I stand. All other ground is sinking sand,' proclaims Terry Butler's musical declaration.

The Apostle Paul was just a man. A man, certainly, who had wonderfully encountered the living, resurrected Christ, a man who had been certain of his own right standing with God through his reputation and standing as an influential Pharisee. But one who now knew that the only sustaining and empowering strength in his life was that of the person of Jesus, Himself. Him alone.

Boy, Paul knew only too well that life that he had previously lived; a life of fervent, religious zeal that involved the persecution, torture and murder of Christian believers. His reputation certainly went before him.

Hence he says:

> "8More than that, I count all things to be loss [c]in view of the surpassing value of [d]knowing Christ Jesus my Lord, [e]for whom I have suffered the loss of all things, and count them but rubbish so that I may gain Christ, 9 and may be found in Him, not having a righteousness of my own derived from the Law, but that which is through faith in Christ, the righteousness which comes from God on the basis of faith, 10 that I may know Him and the power of His resurrection…"
> PHILIPPIANS 3: 8-10

Paul is a man of solid identity, and we need the same assurance and certainty as we invite the Lord to work His purposes in and through us. Only this will keep us through pressures, trials and our own insecurities and mistakes.

Each of us has an 'old life' to reckon as 'dead.' Paul is only too aware of his past life. The life he once held dear and pursued with aggressive purpose now shames him. Or at least it could shame him if he were to let it do so. But no, Paul must reckon that old life to be crucified, gone and 'over' and nothing to do with his newly created life in Jesus Christ. Dead things no longer live. Dead things are disempowered.

MY CHOICE TO BELIEVE

What is it that you have done, or not done, that torments you? What riles you? What nags away at you?

Please hear me. Without wishing in any way to discount or gloss over troubling events and experiences that you may have walked through; may I encourage you to align yourself very deliberately and intentionally with the truth. Applying this truth is going to set you free. Choose the truth of your new identity and heavenly household.

'But I feel so guilty.'
You know, when I am reminded of my many, many failings and even calamitous mistakes – and my wayward part in so many of them – any feelings of guilt and regret must be brought to the Cross. The Cross is not about how guilty I feel. It is about a door at which I choose to lay down my independence, and the consequences that this self-rule has brought.

"Eventually, I surrendered my negative self-image and laid it on God's altar. I chose to stop serving others' opinions of me and the painful memories of my past and to start serving the Lord."

JOAN HUNTER

I repent. I turn and face the other way. I choose life. I choose the truth. I am not going to keep saying sorry to the Lord. Religion might encourage a continuing sense of remorse and the notion that I am somehow 'paying for' my past, at least in some respect. Balancing the books? *'Well, he deserves to feel shame for what happened.' 'I deserve to pay for my deliberate unkindness.'*

God's grace to me is not about what I may or may not deserve.

"Though all that be a fact, you and I can stand now in the presence of God as sinlessly perfect, not in ourselves, but in Christ, as having absolute sinless perfection put to our account by God."

T AUSTIN -SPARKS

The Cross has, once and for all, balanced my books and, more than that, endowed me with a new robe of family belonging and an eternal inheritance of favour, love and provision.

It is completely unfair. Unfair in our favour. Perhaps, a graphic would help.

Sin Record: Steve Hawkins
File not found.

Please note it is not dated. It always applies. The Blood has saved and qualified me forever. You are no different.

It has balanced your books, too, Christian man and woman. It is now for you to live in the generosity of God's heart and to maximise your potential as His ambassador.

That's right – you carry Heaven's calling card. You represent Heaven and its authority. Press into it. Use it. Wield it. Keep your eyes on Jesus, the One who authored your faith and the One who is Omega, bringing it to completion.

"Your life will be a blessed and balanced experience if you first honour your identity and priority."

Russell M. Nelson

4
MISSION POSSIBLE

Fulfilling my mission depends on my mindset. It depends upon my agreeing with the word of God. The Holy Spirit always agrees with the word of God, so I had better agree with Him. Kingdom identity is Jesus' gift to us. Perhaps this illustration will serve to emphasise this.

'ID'

'ID' is a hard-hitting movie from 1995. The film's cover slogan reads *"When you go undercover, remember who you are."*

The film is not alone in standing as a worthy, modern-day parable. Unfortunately, I cannot really recommend it to you on the grounds of its extreme content and unsavoury language, but I trust that the following observations will help.

A police officer is tasked with going undercover among a 'firm' of football hooligans. Success will depend upon his ability to be utterly convincing – all of the time. He is going to need to get his hands dirty. He is going to need to completely embrace the role.

To succeed, he is going to need to *become* the role. Gangs of football hooligans know their own and a flawed performance could place him in serious danger. At least he will not be alone. Three colleagues will make up the rest of this covert unit. But will the four of them be able to pull this off? Does the fact that the four 'coppers' are so well-acquainted pose a threat to this dangerous façade?

Soccer violence rears its head from time to time today, but in the eighties, it was a big deal. In ID, the fictional gang are known to be responsible for much of south London's flare-ups, notwithstanding some non-football-related crime as well. These criminals would be worth busting but it will take some intensive, committed police work.

John, our intrepid secret agent and character lead, is going to feel the pain right from the start. He will need to get the group's trust and in circles such as these, where informants are commonplace, that's not going to be straightforward.

The guys attach themselves to Shadwell Town, the fictional, London club. A movie about football, it isn't. It swiftly becomes a close character study of John's changing behaviour and attitudes which leave the viewer beginning to wonder exactly what is going on and whether John is on an altogether different, rogue journey.

Like the tortured soldier who feigns madness to get a reprieve, until no one is quite sure anymore whether he has actually tripped into a mental spiral or not, John's performance as a hooligan becomes so consistently reprehensible that his colleagues begin to wonder whether he has 'turned.'

The force becomes concerned to the point of discussing pulling the four out. The final scene of the movie is most memorable; a far-right march through the streets of London shows John, in the midst of the marchers, making a Nazi salute. Who is he, now, this young man? Does *he* know who he is?

A CHILD OF THE HOUSE

Many of you will be familiar with the angle often taken by preachers when describing the Biblical tale of the Parable of the Lost Son – namely, that the elder brother had as much to learn about sonship as did his roving, younger sibling.

"I now see that the hands that forgive, console, heal, and offer a festive meal must become my own."

HENRI NOUWEN

The father of that household rejoiced with abandon at the return of his wandering boy and had the older brother shared his father's heart, he would have celebrated, too. We need to remember that Jesus *is the Way* to the Father's heart.

The senior brother's lack of compassion revealed the distance that he was living from his father in a *relational* sense. They might have been geographically under the same roof, but, evidently, the young man was not benefiting from truly knowing the father's heart *for him,* as well as, his deep love for the lust-ridden, younger brother.

Perhaps he – the older one – lived very *correctly*. Perhaps he was also joyless. I have met some very *correct* believers. Have you? They take pride in their scriptural diligence but, I wonder, don't always seem to have found the joy of the Father's house.

Please take this the right way. I have a feeling that when I see the Father, face to face, through streaming tears of delight, He might then suggest we play a game!

We know, don't we, from the parable, that sin brought no genuine joy or contentment to the younger boy. We are not saying, here, that sin brings joy. But estrangement from the father of the house brings dryness and does not represent the father's design for a true relationship.

You have been transferred into the Kingdom of the beloved Father through the precious blood of His Son, Jesus Christ. This was not of your doing, rather it was His initiative. You began with a spiritual birth. Your spiritual development will continue, *always,* as a work of the Holy Spirit.

"Through the Holy Spirit, I have constant access to God. Our battery connection can't go dead. Circuits can't overload. God won't put me on hold, and I don't have to worry about call-waiting."
"My Father is a captive audience to my every thought, my every move. He listens for even the most subtle signs of my spirit stirring…"
SHELLY BEACH

Another movie which is worthy of comment on this issue of belonging is 'The Family Man.'

'I CHOOSE US.'

Permit me to indulge you with another cinematic parable.

'The Family Man' (1995) stars Nicholas Cage (Jack) and Tea Leoni (Kate), a couple very much in love. Well, they once were.

Life can bring critical crossroads, and Jack is offered an opportunity to take a year's placement in London. The couple have talked through the ramifications of the career opening and have decided that Jack should invest this time in his work in financial services. There doesn't appear to be any notable threat to their mutual devotion and it will just be for a year.

However, at the airport, as they embrace their farewell, Kate appears to have a *kairos* moment. Despite their agreement on this extended, temporary parting, Kate urges Jack not to go. She seems to have had a moment of realization that this isn't going to end well. Acknowledging the previous discussions that have led them here, she declares: "I choose us."

In Jack's mind, he is not choosing his career over Kate. This is part of their 'together' life, albeit with a period of geographical distancing. Indeed, he is investing in them both in his mind. Jack leans upon the understanding of his logic and reasoning and leaves a tearful Kate in the airport lounge.

Fast forward to the present, and Jack has clearly moved on. Kate is no more than a distant memory, well and truly receded to the backyard of his ambitions. He is a talented businessman. He is a womaniser. He works, and works, and works. He expects those in his company team to share his relentless work ethic.

In his employment, he is one position, only, below the CEO, a boss who admires Jack for his stamina and reliability and for his devotion to the prime cause that unites them – making money.

Now, this movie is not intrinsically a Christian production but, within the fantasy framework that the medium offers, a spiritual 'someone' of a higher power has been watching Jack and *it matters how he is living his life. It matters that he is not living, or does not belong within, a life of substance.* Jack has not seen what is possible and so, there is going to be an intervention.

For now, we'll call him an angel. There is a moment of meeting when the angel poses as a store thief and is confronted by the well-meaning Jack.

During their exchange, Jack states that "he needs nothing." The fuse has been well and truly lit, and his life is about to change course quite drastically.

Jack goes to bed that night, alone in his hotel room. Accompanied by some 'something weird is about to happen' music, Jack then awakes to find a blonde woman in his bed. A different bed. It's Kate, his almost forgotten love.

Before Jack can even begin to process the apparent mirage, two children and a dog arrive on the bed, too. Sending him downstairs to get a 'strong coffee' – a foreshadowing of the emotional angst that shortly awaits her 'husband', Jack takes a step further. He makes a run for it, assuming that he is in the middle of some kind of hallucinatory trip.

Jumping in the somewhat feeble, family saloon, (the Ferrari is nowhere to be seen,) Jack heads for the office. To safety. To where he surely belongs. But the usually cordial doorman does not know him from Adam, and a colleague, arriving for work, is equally unknowing and dismissive.

Shortly, our angel appears and gives Jack a very short version of what is going on. He is going to get a 'glimpse' of another life. Just a glimpse. There are no time limits and few instructions. Jack will have to work it out as he goes along. *Quelle nightmare.*

May I interject here? Jack has been pretty sure of his identity. He's fast, he plays loose. He knows what he wants, and he takes it. But his place in the world has so much more substance to offer him and he is going to need to adapt quickly.

I see Kate as a Holy Spirit-type figure. The Holy Spirit loves us deeply and has chosen to bless us, to work in our lives, and to form the life of Christ Jesus within us. He is absolutely committed to this work because He knows that it brings much fruit for the Kingdom.

Jack walked away from Kate at the airport, but the movie plot is going to get to work on him at his core level. In his revised dimension, the house is 'alright'. He can barely cope with the two children but begins to warm to them. He discovers that he works as a supervisor, in a cramped downtown office, at a tyre sales company. In this field, the company is a success, and Jack discovers that he has been integral in that.

We, I believe, sometimes think that our sphere of influence should be elsewhere than exactly where the Lord has placed us in His eternal *now*. That grass always looks so much greener on the other side. But is it real grass?

The plot moves effortlessly to bring Jack's pre-glimpse world into a confrontation with his current one when his previous boss stops by for a limousine tyre job. Jack jumps at the chance to reacquaint himself with the CEO and immediately impresses him with his business banter and air of confidence. He is invited to drop the limo off himself once the job has been completed.

Jack's foot is in the door. And, of course, he has the advantage of knowing all about the business and its employees. One of his subordinates now holds Jack's role in the boardroom and as Jack is invited to a meeting with the two heavyweights, Jack knows that he has to play his cards carefully, but confidently.

It might be my favourite scene of the movie; owning the space in the room as the two bosses sit closely together on a sofa, Jack 'reads' the two men from his years of experience of working with them, describing their eating and drinking habits, tastes in life, the whole lot.

As the CEO smiles appreciatively, realising the talent in the room, Alan, the character who now has Jack's position, shifts increasingly uncomfortably in his seat, no doubt very aware that this newcomer could outgun him at will.

Jack is hired, and with the new position comes a new, healthy salary, not to mention the opportunity to move into a spanking new, spacious apartment. Jack feels that he is 'coming home.' But it's not going to be a smooth transition.

Surprising Kate with the news as he takes her to view the new residence, her reaction is not what Jack has hoped for. Moving here would mean leaving the country neighbourhood for the city, moving the children from their schools and Kate leaving her own job, one that she loves from her heart.

Jack's frustrations at her reactions only serve to bring Kate's true feelings to the surface. "People would so envy us here!" pleads Jack. "Oh Jack. They already do." She has long seen and appreciated the true value of their life together. Her identity is secure and at rest. She knows, perfectly, where she belongs.

Jack is making decisions out of brokenness, while Kate's sure foundation of who she is, albeit in a world of limited finance and opportunity, stands out starkly. Jack needs this *stuff* while Kate appreciates that any such extras are only a sprinkling upon the essence of who she really is, a devoted wife and mother with a valued circle of genuine friends. She has other talents, too, which are soon to be revealed.

The movie had prepared us for this exchange a little earlier, when, upon a weekend visit to a store, Jack had wandered into 'menswear' and espied a smart, casual jacket, crafted to the kind of quality that he had regularly sported in his previous life. While Kate's idea of a weekend treat is to buy some cake, Jack expresses his 'need' to spend over $200 on this item. Kate makes the point well – does he truly need this to feel like he is someone of worth? Jack declares that he "actually feels a better person" while wearing the jacket.

But Jack is progressing. His relationship with Kate grows, he sees her strength and inner beauty, as well as her obvious, outer shine. Relaxing more in the home has brought him closer to the children. Jack is settling.

Another meeting with our angel guy is about to change all that. Angel explains that his time is up and reminds Jack that this was, after all, only a glimpse. Jack's protests are about to fall on deaf ears.

The next morning, he wakes up alone in that hotel bed, once again. But he *is* a transformed man – he cannot deny what he has seen and the richness of what he has experienced *en famille*. He believes that he truly belongs there. He decides to try to track down Kate.

Tea Leoni excels as the two meet at her art shop; she is slick, confident, assured. Polite to the rather orphaned-looking Jack, she speaks to him almost professionally; she is courteous but there is no warmth. He is reaching out to her but failing to make a connection. Indeed, she is busily going about her tasks even as Jack, bemused, fumbles his way through the encounter.

Kate is packing up. She's going to Paris. She clearly has a new life and a new vision ahead of her. But Jack has now seen too much. He is going to fight for her, now, as hard as he ever did for a business deal.

Come the critical moment. Hearing that Kate has left for the airport, Jack hurtles to the venue in a final, desperate effort to save his 'dream come reality.' Catching her right at the gate, Kate, again, shows little interest except to assure him that he has the closure he might be looking for.

Jack turns away, but he has one, last move. He calls out again and, this time, describes their family, their life, and their children. As Kate stares at him, a spark of recognition is lit in her heart and the truth, the realness of Jack's words seems to find a place in her understanding.

The end scene showing the couple having coffee together, Kate having ceded to delay her flight to France, suggests that they are, once again, choosing each other over all other agendas.

Failing to appropriate God's word and His provision, can lead us to a significant identity crisis.

HIROO ONODA

Hiroo Onoda was a Japanese serviceman and a hero in folklore. Enlisted into the Japanese Imperial Army during the Second World War, Onoda was trained in covert espionage and propaganda. He was posted to the Philippines in 1945 as part of a unit that would disrupt the progress of the Allies, especially with operations around harbours and landing strips.

The Allies invaded in February 1945 and most Japanese soldiers were either killed or evacuated. But not Onoda. Onoda had received an order from a superior officer to the end that he should, under all circumstances, 'hold his ground' and never surrender.

That was the last order Onoda was to receive. Even as he was aware that his comrades were leaving the islands and that he, himself, would be picked up within a definite period of time, he knew that this order was irrevocable. He would obey it.

Onoda knew nothing of the Japanese surrender on August 15th. This ignorance was to change the man's identity for another *thirty* years. He believed that he was required to continue to serve, as at war, when he wasn't.

How tragic. In 1974, Onoda was still in the Philippines. He had ignored leaflet drops over the islands, assuring him that the war was long over. Why should he, a trained operative in espionage and propaganda, believe such nonsense?

You know, our spiritual enemy has watched us since birth. He knows our strengths and our weaknesses. He is livid that he has lost legal right to us and can now only do his best to deceive us and to keep our hearts shrouded in religious bondage and lies. If he can keep us trying to earn what we have already been given, he may reduce our effectiveness as we seek to be ambassadors for the Kingdom of Light.

I know that God wants us free – free in the liberty of Christ Jesus! Onoda did, eventually, come into his own freedom. A Japanese explorer, Norio Suzuki, set out on an expedition to find Onoda and on February 27th 1974, he located him. But that wasn't quite the end of it. Onoda would still not leave until he saw a signed release from a superior officer. He certainly was a man of honour and a man of his word.

We may be presented with the truth about our standing in Jesus Christ many times before the penny drops and we see – we understand – that Christ has released us from our former way of thinking and birthed us into new life. There needs to be a revelation from the Holy Spirit. The things of the spirit are spiritually discerned.

MASKS AND MAYHEM

The Holy Spirit is passionate about each of us and works to support our progress in Kingdom identity. When He says, '*I choose us,*' He really means it – He is a covenant-keeping God and His word is unequivocally His word.

To what extent we partner with Him in this transformation and outworking of heavenly purpose probably varies hugely. Life happens. We are faithless.

We are faithful. We are open to the Lord, open with unguarded vulnerability, at times. At other times, we may feel we have shut down.

But the Alpha and Omega is not phased. He has His way around and His way through.
He chose us and today He still chooses us. Today there is a way forward and He is already there. His steps have already imprinted our future ground.

The enemy of His purposes will try to distract, discourage and dismay us. He will lie to us, and try to convince us that our good, good Father is heartless and distant. He will accuse the Lord in our ears and will accuse us in own ears, too. He will provide hours and hours of entertainment, perhaps a few dopamine-inducing doses of popularity that require us to deviate just a little from who we really are.

The masking buzz may drive us and provide a ride for a while. It may even lead us into mayhem as we become aware that the most precious element of our lives has receded from our regular, everyday experience.

The presence of God. He is our best friend, our warmth, our strength, our home. We may realise that we have taken a trip, just like that younger, biblical brother. The Holy Spirit shows the same passion for us, today, as does the Father each time we meet Him in that parable.

The final scene of 'Family Man' shows Jack and Kate talking animatedly together. Here we are at the end of a movie that has seen business meetings, family mess, mental stress and confusion, temptation, ambition – and the list goes on. The simplicity of eye-to-eye contact and conversation is a good reminder, I think, of the opportunities that we have to grow in our friendship and love of the Holy Spirit. He chooses us.

"I pledge allegiance to the Christian flag, and to the Savior, for whose Kingdom it stands, one Savior, crucified, risen, and coming again, with life and liberty for all who believe."

Dan Quayle

5
RULERS SIT

> "¹¹Every priest stands daily ministering and offering time after time the same sacrifices, which can never take away sins; ¹² but He, having offered one sacrifice for [f]sins for all time, sat down at the right hand of God, ¹³ waiting from that time onward until His enemies be made a footstool for His feet. ¹⁴ For by one offering He has perfected for all time those who are [g]sanctified."
> HEBREWS 10:12

A war has been fought. The victor has won. He sits down, in the aftermath of battle, to receive acclaim and to demonstrate His position of authority. There would usually be a celebratory feast in the presence of the defeated foe.

So where are we? Are we seated, too?

> "⁴But God, being rich in mercy, because of His great love with which He loved us, ⁵ even when we were dead [f]in our transgressions, made us alive together [g]with Christ (by grace you have been saved), ⁶ and raised us up with Him, and seated us with Him in the heavenly places in Christ Jesus, ⁷ so that in the ages to come He might show the surpassing riches of His grace in kindness toward us in Christ Jesus. ⁸ For by grace you have been saved through faith; and [h]that not of yourselves, it is the gift of God; ⁹ not as a result of works, so that no one may boast. ¹⁰ For we are His workmanship, created in Christ Jesus for good works, which God prepared beforehand so that we would walk in them."
> EPHESIANS: 2 4-9 – emphasis added

The purpose of our position is also stated clearly; that Christ may show us grace, grace to all, who would receive Him. Grace to us. Grace demonstrated through us.

Also, to show that He is so kind and has bestowed a gift upon us – it is not from ourselves – it is not due to our works, whatever their quality. Boasting is irrelevant and nothing, in this supernatural, heavenly transaction. Boasting simply does not belong, as a fly would not in the most precious ointment.

Though we may boast in Him, our supreme Lord and benefactor (2 Corinthians 12). The good works that we have been created for – saved for – are available to us and all that we need to play our part has been provided for us.

The religious spirit will baulk at this and demand that self-effort contributes, that somehow, there might be an element of the self, deserving such lavish grace and kindness shown it. Self needs to be acknowledged – it craves attention and validation.

But we cannot add to a finished work. We can but participate in it, enjoy it, embrace it and spread the news that the Lord is alive and is still distributing salvation and healing to all who will embrace Him.

THEOLOGY ALIVE

Our position in Jesus Christ is something far more vital and life-changing than a mental assent to a theological doctrine. Do we think that the abundant life that Jesus talks about is purely a mental formula or intellectual exhilaration? And what about the eternity of the Bible? Is He only talking about the prospect of a place in Heaven when our earthly life has ended?

If we were chosen before the foundation of the world – if we were sealed into Christ Jesus – if we have already been seated in Heaven with Him – then our life has become an extraordinary, supernatural adventure.

I'm not suggesting that this necessarily equates to worldwide renown or uncountable thrills per second for ourselves. Is that what we want? Don't we long for His worldwide renown? Our lives may or may not become evident in the public eye, but the world's attention cannot sit amongst our dearest priorities.

Will we lay down our expectations of what our lives may hold? If God has spoken to you, if He has confirmed plans and direction for you, then marvellous. I have many promises over my life which are yet to be fulfilled. I hold them lightly. I hold them before Him and unto Him. He is the Lord, and this journey is about His glory.

Isn't it stunning that He speaks to us? He doesn't need to explain or justify Himself to anyone. He demonstrates that very well through His words to Job.

> "7 Now gird up your loins like a man; I will ask you, and you instruct Me.
> 8 Will you really annul My judgment? Will you condemn Me that you may be justified?
> 9 Or do you have an arm like God, And can you thunder with a voice like His?"
> JOB 40:7-9

At the same time, having become His friends, He does love to share His heart with us and to encourage us to walk in the directional light that we have. He will be delighted to correct us should we begin to veer off course. We will hear a voice behind us saying "This is the way, walk in it," (Isaiah 30). We might need to wait. We will need to stay in His rest.

Rest comes from that position of sitting with Him. We sit, knowing that we forever belong.

FOR HIM

For we are His workmanship. This workmanship will be fit for His purposes. I wonder how many times you have missed the mark, missed the way, missed the turning? Perhaps you think you've really messed up your calling. Perhaps things have not turned out at all as you thought or hoped they might. I imagine this is just about everyone's story to some degree or another.

But, today you are alive. Today you are in the company of the Holy Spirit who is the redeemer. There is nothing too hard for Him to turn His mighty hands to. As we remember, once again, that we are about *His* purposes and not our own – God will move and *again* show us His boundless creativity.

We're going to have to trust Him, aren't we? Is there an alternative? Would we lay our bets on anyone else than God? The God who demonstrates his untiring love and faithfulness. The One who knows us as no one else could know us.

We're going to have 'off' days. Bad days. Tough circumstances. Sometimes we might blow it. Speak out of turn. Be unkind. Make no mistake that the enemy of our lives – the jealous, fallen archangel – will jump into action and accuse us of our hopelessness and blotched track record.

'You're just not reliable. You're unstable. You'll screw up again. Why would God trust you? Why would God give responsibilities to someone so flawed?' Because this 'one' belongs to Him and He who began a good work in me is unnerved and very much on the job. It was never about us producing a perfect performance. It always was about Jesus Christ being glorified in these frail, earthy vessels.

Earthy, but filled with the very Spirit of God. I think it is the author, Eugene Peterson, who has a scene in one of his books in which watching angels marvel at the unthought-of move of God – to fill fallen humans with His precious Life. I hope our self-esteem is getting an upgrade.

REAL HUMILITY

I think the best and simplest definition of humility I have come across is this: knowing who God is and knowing who we are designed to be in Him. Humility needs to add nothing more to that equation. Religious behaviour or people-pleasing will not work. Bashing ourselves emotionally for our flaws and misjudgements may tender the flavour of godly devotion but such a response is not based in truth.

"What is genuine self-love? It is not self-exaltation; it is self-acceptance and appreciation for who God has made you to be…you know who you are. It is no longer an issue."

DAN SNEED

Humility bows low and accepts the work of the Cross in our lives. Humility prefers God and, as He leads, prefers one another over oneself. Humility stands tall before the Lord, too. Sons and daughters understand the power of their family name and the favour of their loving Overseer and Shepherd.

They understand the reality of their redeeming rescue. They birth compassion for others who have yet to discover it – many of these dear people having served in the Church for many years. Something changes when you know – really know – that you *belong*. Those who belong will sit.

One of the first things we do when we invite someone to our homes, surely, is to welcome them and offer them a chair. We are demonstrating their right to be here, to be at ease, to be at peace. We show them that they are valued simply for being themselves. We want them in our presence. And there is a good chance that they will be offered a drink and perhaps some food.

> "[20]Behold, I stand at the door and knock; if anyone hears My voice and opens the door, I will come in to him and will dine with him, and he with Me."
> REVELATION 3:20

Not only that. Remember what other behaviour Jesus demonstrated when welcoming His disciples. Didn't he wash their feet? Didn't He – the Lord of the Universe – serve them?

In my humility before the Lord, I choose to hold my head up high. He has lifted me from the depths. He has lifted me from gutter behaviour and a bunch of ungodly beliefs. He has shown me the bondage that religion and legalism bring. He has decreed me qualified for eternal life and to play a part in His 'ministry of reconciliation.'

The Psalms declare God's pleasure with His people.

> "As for the [a]saints who are in the earth, [b]They are the majestic ones in whom is all my delight."
> PSALM 16:3

I bow, I have been seated and I stand in Jesus Christ.

"The Bible says that our real problem is that every one of us is building our identity on something besides Jesus."
Timothy Keller

6
ON EARTH, AS IT IS IN HEAVEN

For how long have we prayed – perhaps even mechanically recited – this phrase from what is commonly known as The Lord's Prayer?

The Lord's Prayer. I don't really think that Jesus ever meant this to be a 'set prayer,' as such. "Show us how to pray, Lord," the disciples asked Him, (Luke 11). In other words, how can our prayers be effective, powerful, influential, *in authority*?

As Jesus teaches them, He gives them keys to their approach to the Father: He *is* their Father, first off, and He is in Heaven. What a glorious revelation. We come with worship – 'Hallowed' or 'to be honoured as holy,' is Your unique, magnificent name, the Name above all names.

We align ourselves and our motives and desires with Heaven's, Kingdom purpose.
"Thy Kingdom come, Thy will be done on earth, as it is in Heaven."
The ramifications of praying in this way are colossal. The Kingdom of God is unrivalled in Heaven and every purpose of the Lord is being exercised in perfection.

Temporarily, the earth realm (and, of course, Revelation speaks of a 'new' earth realm to come,) is under alien, evil management – destructive, dark and demonic. The fruit of such spiritual oversight is clear for all to see, in people's personal lives, a country's national life, and also internationally, all over the world. Newspapers and today's round-the-clock newscasts keep us abreast of the turmoil.

Sick trees produce sick fruit, (Matthew 7). Always. But, in terms of our current earth realm, that's not even half the story. Upon this earth, beautifully created by our wonderful, designer God, yet flawed by the consequences of sin and a loss of spiritual authority, the Lord is, nevertheless, flawlessly working out and fulfilling His purposes and employing the resources of His Church as a means of doing so. We get to join in, not just watch.

Just how powerful is this prayer made in the name of Jesus Christ, the Lord of Lords and King of Kings?
"Father, let this be on earth as it is in Heaven."
All of Heaven's resources are brought about to agree with and to enforce the decree of such a prayer. Father acts, Jesus exercises His authority, the Holy Spirit takes the wheel in unruly circumstances and angels are assigned to confirm the Lord's activity.

Might the prayer be contested? Might Hell and its demonic cohorts resist? Quite probably, but at some stage, to some degree and often completely, this opposition will yield. It will give way.
The enemy knows when a Christian is praying in *His* faith, in the faith that understands Kingdom authority.

ADVANCING

The truth is that the Kingdom that we are part of - and our place in its progress and dominion – is not on the back foot. And we are not spare parts. The Bible says that even the least of us are greater than John the Baptist! That's a clear marker of the importance of our identity in Jesus.

[11] "Truly I say to you, among those born of women there has not arisen *anyone* greater than John the Baptist! Yet the one who is [m]least in the kingdom of heaven is greater than he. [12] From the days of John the Baptist until now the kingdom of heaven [n]suffers violence, and violent men [o]take it by force."

> "From the days of John the Baptist until now, the kingdom of heaven has been advancing forcefully and forceful people are seizing it." - The Holy Bible, English Heritage Version
> MATTHEW 11:12

God's Kingdom has been won by Christ as a prize. The victory of the Cross has assured the Kingdom of God the presence and progress of the precious Church that you and I are part of. We are prize winners, not through our own efforts, by no means. Our Champion, Jesus Christ, has done the complete work.

Our part is to 'seize' the Kingdom. As the enemy tried to usurp the Kingdom and was eternally punished for doing so, we, on the other hand, get to grip the Kingdom under the lordship of Christ and partner with Him as He establishes His purposes on earth, *as it is in heaven.*

Praying that earth will see Kingdom order and rule, as it is in Heaven, is a mighty way to pray. On any level. Concerning anything and anyone. Is any situation excluded? I am praying for a loved one who is ill, let's say. We know that we have the authority, in Jesus Christ, to pray for the sick and to see healing. This is His word. The Cross's purpose has been fulfilled – all sin and sickness have been dealt with and their authority nullified.

Healing manifests itself in many ways and, often, in unseen ways which we struggle to fathom. But God says, "Pray," "Lay hands on the sick and they will recover". I wonder what your and my next opportunity will be to do just that. As we are led by the Holy Spirit, He will open up those opportunities.

As we live 'in the way' as Paul describes it, it won't always be the right time to pray. It may be that the Spirit of God will cause you to pause – perhaps there is other work for Him to do before praying can bring about His desires.

Unsure of how to pray, I can pray an awesome prayer, nevertheless, 'Father, in the name of Jesus Christ, I decree heaven's divine order on earth.'

The Lord may show you other ways to pray. Praying in tongues is a glorious weapon, a piece of heavenly, supernatural equipment. Paul rates this gift very highly.

> "⁵Now I wish that you all spoke in tongues …"
> 1 CORINTHIANS 14:5

Praying in tongues is always a wonderful reminder that we are dealing with and living in a spiritual, supernatural realm. In Ephesians, Paul reminds us that 'flesh and blood' are not going to effectively deal with issues that are located in the heavenly realms.

> "¹²For our struggle is not against [a]flesh and blood, but against the rulers, against the powers, against the world forces of this darkness, against the spiritual *forces* of wickedness in the heavenly *places*…"
> EPHESIANS 6:12

Perhaps the Lord has placed a nation on your heart. You know when it's the Lord who is doing that. That deep, warm desire to pray and intercede goes much further than your own reasoning and understanding.

I can pray 'in the Spirit' – the Holy Spirit is always aligned to the will of the Father. I can pray with the understanding that I feel He has given me. And I can pray that God will exercise His desire and authority in that place, as He has purposed from Heaven.

> "I want to emphasise the utterly different conception of things which obtains in heaven. Their standards are so altogether different from ours, ways of looking at things, and yet the Lord Jesus goes as far as to say that that mind should come down here, that mentality should be expressed here, those standards should be established here."
> T AUSTIN SPARKS

And Jesus, the heart of the Christian faith is the wildest, most radical guy you'd ever come across.

Bear Grylls

7
HEAVEN – GLORIOUS DESTINATION AND OUR BASE NOW

Heaven is not just the wished-for 'end of the road' destination for the believer in Jesus.

I pray that the Holy Spirit will enlighten and encourage you as you imbibe the contents of this chapter.

I imagine that even many solid believers would say that going to Heaven is the beginning of our eternal life with Christ. My faith means that I am saved now – ticket booked – while Heaven is for later. We have already seen that we have been seated in heaven with Christ, (Ephesians 2). I believe the Bible; therefore I accept that I am seated with Jesus, *now*. Heaven is for now.

True, the fulfilment of our eternal destiny in Heaven will continue once each of us leaves this temporary home called 'Now Earth'. It is true, too, that we do not yet see even a smidgen of the total reality of this Kingdom place. But we have seen some things. They have been revealed to us by the Holy Spirit.

Holy Spirit loves to reveal to us. He loves to share! You would think by the manner in which some describe the final book in our Bible, Revelation, that the book was rather titled 'Hidden'.

We are His friends now. We are sons and daughters of His house. His house is the Kingdom of Heaven and we are actually seated there, now. Right now. To the person who says, so wisely it may seem, that we 'should not get too heavenly minded or we will be of no earthly good,' `I politely reply, 'No way.' I would suggest that the very opposite is true.

We are heavenly people in Christ Jesus with a limited period of time on Now Earth; during this 'stay' we deepen our friendship with the Lord and allow Him to express Himself through our lives. That's part of evangelism; not only the proclamation of the gospel truth, but the evidence of it expressed in our lives.

God also knows exactly how many days we each have to spend on 'Now Earth'.

> "And in Your book were all written The days that were ordained *for me*, When as yet there was not one of them."
> PSALM 139:16

In the book of Acts, we read that the Holy Spirit came upon the disciples, as promised by Jesus and as prophesied in the Old Testament (Joel 2), to empower them and to enable them to fulfil Kingdom business on earth *now*. This witness to the world would begin locally and then spread, spread through the nation and onwards to every nation. Even to the 'remotest part of the earth.' They were instructed to wait for this release of power because their own strength would not have been appropriate for the mission. You and I are witnesses of Jesus Christ. Witnesses see, they experience. They get to testify to what they have witnessed.

THE REALITY OF HEAVEN

Heaven is real. We belong there. We are seated there, now. Heaven is our base of operation. It has to be if we are going to partner with the Kingdom that is based there. Recognising Kingdom perspective is a huge key to our valuing our time on Now Earth and delighting in the prospect of our future, eternal home.

We are going home. At a time of God's choosing, we return home. Folks – this is real, not a pipe dream. I say 'return,' because according to the word of God, we were born from Heaven in the first place. God tells Jeremiah:

> "Before I formed you in the womb I knew you, And before you were born I consecrated you; I have appointed you a prophet to the nations."
> JEREMIAH 1:5

Having this perspective as to the reality of who we truly are in Christ will gird us, empower and motivate us.

The realities of Heaven and its realms are being revealed to countless believers these days; many had never expected to be made so aware of them; others have asked for such revelation and received it in prayer and in dreams. I would so love to have more.

I am deliciously grateful for the comparatively small glimpses I have known. Shortly after becoming a Christian at the University of Birmingham in the UK, I had a small series of experiences of the supernatural presence of God. I have never forgotten them. I doubt I ever will.

When God does something in your life, He uses the only currency that reflects His person and character – e*ternity*. Everything He does is effective and it lasts. It cannot be undone. It becomes part of who you are. As a cordial is mixed with water and the two have become inseparable, so are God's works in our lives.

I think – as far as I can understand as I look back at those college years and the subsequent ones that followed, that God graciously allowed me to see the reality of Heaven as a tool to support me through some hugely tough times. He is eternal and operates in eternity. He is the great I AM but also sees the steps ahead of us and intervenes as He wishes.

Knowing that Heaven is real makes a massive difference to our attitude when there is suffering, pain, bewilderment or loss. It's a *knowing* that I can barely describe to you. I just know. I am sure. Hebrews tells us that faith is the *substance* of things hoped for; it is real substance – tangible, spiritual stuff. In fact, faith is more solid and trustworthy than anything temporal I could mention.

People often seem to associate faith with doubting. Are you in faith? 'I'm going to do this in faith,' often translated as really meaning, 'I don't really know what I'm doing but I think I'm going to do it anyway.' That's not faith.

Faith comes from God. He has faith – He is faith. We receive of Him. Faith is an intimate impartation from Jesus Christ. When we have received from Him, we are not swinging from side to side. We are still. We are sure. We are certain. We are at rest.

"Now faith is the [a]assurance of *things* [b]hoped for, the [c]conviction of things not seen."

> "Faith is being sure about what we hope for, being convinced about things we do not see." - The Holy Bible, Evangelical Heritage version
> HEBREWS 11:1

Yes, I am convinced about Heaven. I have received my hope from Him. I remember hearing a wonderful illustration of what real faith looks like – faith that is substance, faith that is an assurance. I'm not even sure if the story is real or fictional.

A lady with an injury takes a taxi to a Christian healing meeting; she is desperate to be healed and is going to ask for prayer. She is dropped at the doors by the taxi and she instructs the driver to pick her up three hours later. This lady is not in faith. I am sure she is hoping, but that isn't His faith.

A week later, after seeking the Lord and spending some time with Him, she is sure that the Lord has spoken to her. Healing is hers. It isn't that the Lord *could* do it, she knows in her deepest place that He *will* do it.

She calls up the taxi company and they drop her off at the doors of the church building, as before. Only this time, she doesn't order a later pick-up. She knows she is going to get the bus home. That is real faith. May we all have His faith as to the reality of Heaven.

PERHAPS WE ALL KNOW

Go into any waiting room (the picture is quite apt) and you are likely to find a stack of holiday brochures among the fashion, home and sports offerings. Open one up. You have done it, I'm sure. Drink in the enticing, colour-perfect photographs of the 'other world' that the page is promising you.

Mind you, in today's digital, AI world, I wonder to what degree we might trust any of them. See the scenery. Breath-taking, isn't it? The prospect of several days away in 'different' accommodation. It's different. It seems more luxurious, more lavish, more special. *I will feel like a different person staying there.*

Bright lights, bustling markets, sleepy ambling in the countryside or the soft, lapping sea. And – for some – the promise of romance? Of meeting someone, maybe? These inner longings simply point me to the coming reality for the believer. We are going home to a perfect place and will spend eternity with the Perfect One and with His perfected company.

The brochure has succeeded and we pack. We plan. We expect. We dream. We begin to role-play some of it, perhaps. And with such detail and care! Yet – we are only going for a fortnight. How can we extend the adventure? Add in a few excursions? Of course, count in the travel time. Holidays absolutely include the travel time, right?

As a child, the night before our summer holiday was just a little magical – and we went camping every year, pretty much! It was magical because the current place and time were about to be superimposed with something unseen, unexperienced, only imaginable.

Our drive to Wales or the Lake District or Scotland would begin in the early hours of the morning. Mum or Dad would wake us up while it was still dark. How exciting. The air would have an early chill to it. Blurry eyes would give heed to last-minute packing and a spot of breakfast before Dad hitched up the tent trailer and we were set to go.

But, wait. This was for a two-week holiday. When we finally leave 'Now Earth' for Heaven, *we are not coming back*. Our eternal life and its experiences will all stem from our home. Home is where the Father is. Jesus told His disciples and tells us that He is preparing this place for us, (John 14.)

The prospects described in those holiday magazines and brochures connect with our desires for what is perfect. We know that the perfect is 'out there.' Christians are learning that the 'perfect' is in Him.

How carefully – with what focus and excitement – do we peruse the opportunities and beckoning of a holiday heaven? We check every detail, we study each photograph, we begin to imagine our presence in the pictures.

How about perusing some absolute truth about our eternal home? Its qualities will not depend on the weather, crowds, or facilities that are functioning at the time.

REALITY

> "¹Then I saw a new heaven and a new earth; for the first heaven and the first earth passed away, and there is no longer any sea. ² And I saw the holy city, new Jerusalem, coming down out of heaven from God, made ready as a bride adorned for her husband. ³ And I heard a loud voice from the throne, saying, "Behold, the tabernacle of God is among men, and He will [a]dwell among them, and they shall be His people, and God Himself will be among them[b], ⁴ and He will wipe away every tear from their eyes; and there will no longer be any death; there will no longer be any mourning, or crying, or pain; the first things have passed away."
> REVELATION 21: 1-4

Death will not even be a memory there – it will be an unknown, non-existent thing. There is no sadness there, no weeping, no regret and no pain. No pain of any kind whatsoever.
This is a new order. The new, divine order.

The political world speaks of a New World Order but that is an impossible dream without the One who is order. He is perfect order. Fallen men, even those with the noblest of motives, can never make it a reality.

The old things have passed away. Sin nature and its independent, selfish, wilful circumstances will have gone. Shalom – true Shalom – will reign because Jesus is the true Shalom – the deepest, richest sense of well-being that can be experienced.

The New Jerusalem, a sparkling, gleaming city of peace and friendship with Christ Jesus as its head, will compose God and His beloved people, living together in perfect arrangement.

We do well to remember that this city is a real city. John sees it in a vision in Revelation 2. Peruse it, if you will, as you would that brochure. Drink in the detail. I wonder if you can even begin to truly picture its beauty. Perhaps the Holy Spirit will show you some things as you read:

"[10]And he carried me away [g]in the Spirit to a great and high mountain, and showed me the holy city, Jerusalem, coming down out of heaven from God, [11] having the glory of God. Her [h]brilliance was like a very costly stone, as a stone of crystal-clear jasper. [12] [i]It had a great and high wall, [j]with twelve gates, and at the gates twelve angels; and names were written on them, which are the names of the twelve tribes of the sons of Israel. [13] There were three gates on the east and three gates on the north and three gates on the south and three gates on the west. [14] And the wall of the city had twelve foundation stones, and on them were the twelve names of the twelve apostles of the Lamb. [15] The one who spoke with me had a [k]gold measuring rod to measure the city, and its gates and its wall. [16] The city is laid out as a square, and its length is as great as the width; and he measured the city with the [l]rod, [m]fifteen hundred miles; its length and width and height are equal. [17] And he measured its wall, [n]seventy-two yards, according to human [o]measurements, which are also angelic measurements. [18] The material of the wall was jasper; and the city was pure gold, like [p]clear glass. [19] The foundation stones of the city wall were adorned with every kind of precious stone. The first foundation stone was jasper; the second, sapphire; the third, chalcedony; the fourth, emerald; [20] the fifth, sardonyx; the sixth, sardius; the seventh, chrysolite; the eighth, beryl; the ninth, topaz; the tenth, chrysoprase; the eleventh, jacinth; the twelfth, amethyst. [21] And the twelve gates were twelve pearls; each one of the gates was a single pearl. And the street of the city was pure gold, like transparent glass. [22] I saw no [q]temple in it, for the Lord God the Almighty and the Lamb are its [r]temple. [23] And the city has no need of the sun or of the moon to shine on it, for the glory of God has illumined it, and its lamp is the Lamb. [24] The nations will walk by its light, and the kings of the earth [s]will bring their glory into it. [25] In the daytime (for there will be no night there) its gates will never be closed;[26] and they will bring the glory and the honor of the nations into it; [27] and nothing unclean, and no one who practices abomination and lying, shall ever come

into it, but only those [t]whose names are written in the Lamb's book of life.
REVELATION 21: 10-27

This is home. It is the nation of our citizenship, the Kingdom of Heaven. It is brilliant, according to the witness, John. Like me, you may not recognise some of the materials that constitute the city; perhaps you are unaware of the array of stunning colours contained within them.

The foundations alone are almost too perfect to imagine. Of course, it is a perfect foundation, just as Jesus Himself is the perfect and only foundation stone upon which the Kingdom is built.

Jasper – a deep red; sapphire – a soothing yet vibrant blue; chalcedony can vary in its hues but a rich brown or bluey-green may imbibe the third foundation stone. Then we have emerald – another shade of green with hints of blue and/or yellow; sardonyx is a ruddy, orangey red while sardius can range from a pale orange to an almost black.

The remaining six foundations are just as spectacular. Chrysolite is often a pale green or yellow shade while beryl offers a range of options, including pinks, greens and blues. Topaz has a very wide range of colour possibilities and probably includes a shade of just about everything.

How rich! Chrysoprase is often an apple green colour but can also show turquoise and a deeper green, while jacinth contains reds and browns and yellows. The final foundation, amethyst is a bold purple – how appropriate for a royal city, home to the King of Kings and a royal priesthood of believers.

A priesthood which began with the twelve apostles. Their names are eternally visible on the city's foundations. John has seen this exquisite vision 'coming down' so all the colours of the foundations have been before his eyes.

The city is a four-sided figure, the points of the compass clearly designated with a set of gates on each of the four sides; twelve, pearl gates stand, each recording a name of one of the twelve tribes of Israel. One day. One, heavenly day I am going to see these gates. They're in Heaven's brochure.

STREETS OF GOLD

Perhaps one of the most classic and memorable ideas of a place called Paradise, is that the streets should be made of gold. Disney might want to reproduce it or another of the well-known film studios. A wonderful, unique, utopian city where everyone lives perfectly together in absolute peace; a place where the very nature and flavour of conflict are unknown and would never be recognized let alone understood.

How could it be present, in any vestige, when the Kingdom is ruled by the Prince of Peace, who is Light and in whom there is no darkness at all, (1 John 5)? I am fascinated by this passage in Revelation.

Complete a quick street survey and most people would say that gold is a yellowy-gold colour. Gold gets its colour from the impurities within it. The finest gold that we can buy today has colour. Only the very purest gold – 100% pure gold – is colourless.

There is no impurity of any kind in Heaven. Hence, we read that the gold streets are as 'clear glass.' John saw this – he testifies to it. Our biblical brochure describes the very streets that we will walk on. John relays what he witnesses; I don't know if John was knowledgeable about the nature and quality of gold; he uses the language he best can and those streets are perfect. Perhaps he receives a little help from his tour guide, 'the one who spoke with me,' (Revelation 21)

Don't you just love the idea, too, of streets? It is truly a city, a place of living and life, of relationship and transaction and secure dwelling. Revelation is designed to reveal and so John's visionary account states clearly that the city is laid out in the shape of an exact square. Human measurements are used to enlighten us – and, I would suggest, stagger us with their ramifications.

Not only that, but its height is also as long as its breath and width! Some have suggested a cuboid-type structure, in this event. The city is 1500 miles long. And wide. And high.
1500 miles. That's about the distance between London and Moscow. Or New York and Austin. One city.

There will be no police force in Heaven because the city is totally secure; there is no darkness, no decay, no rebellion, no violence. We are told that the walls of the city are 'seventy-two yards' in thickness; that's in the region of sixty-five metres. This supernatural city for supernatural people and angelic beings is of an essence that we have not envisaged.

CHRIST – THE TEMPLE

John is shown a city, one with streets and gates and walls. But there is no temple. Why would Heaven need a temple built by human hands or by human design? Jesus, Himself, is the living temple – the perfect object of worship – He is the very place where worship is drawn to, accepted and enjoyed.

What was the purpose of the magnificent, awe-inspiring temple that graced Jerusalem and that was seen as such a prize to be captured by the Lord's enemies?

> "One [thing] have I desired of the LORD, that will I seek after; that I may dwell in the house of the LORD all the days of my life, to behold the beauty of the LORD, and to inquire in his temple."
> PSALM 27:4

The temple was a holy place where the Jews could learn of, worship and pray to their God; the One who had taken them as His own, treasured possession. 'To behold the beauty of the Lord;' that is the purpose of the temple.

In Heaven, eyes delight in the beauty of the Lord who is present among His people. On earth, magnificently constructed and furnished buildings have sought to reflect His worth and glory. In Heaven, reflections are replaced with the reality – the reality Himself. Stunning. We belong to Him. He is ours and we are His. Such incomparable glory needs no backup or support. There is no deficit in any sense.

So, not even the sun is required. Not here. Jesus Christ, Himself, radiates such indescribable power, light and purity that He alone illumines the Kingdom. I say, He alone. What do I know? A Kingdom where the Father, Son and Holy Spirit reside, and rule houses no darkness at all.

This is a place of light, in every conceivable sense of the word.

> "⁵This is the message we have heard from Him and announce to you, that God is Light, and in Him there is no darkness at all."
> 1 JOHN 1:5

Freedom. Transparency. Understanding. The purest of love and intimacy. Divine order.
We will be part of a divine order in which the nations look to and are embraced by the Lord of Lords and His majestic love. Can we really even begin to imagine such a society? It is real. We are going to be part of it.

> "The Lord has come down here. He is the heavenly standard; He is the governing weight and measure of God's thought. You can only know the Lord Jesus by revelation of the Holy Spirit. He is not someone to be imitated from without. He is to be known only as the Spirit of God shows us. He was here, but they did not understand why He did this and that and refused to do this and that. An accepted thing among religious people, and yet He would not have it, He would not go when they wanted Him to go, and they did not understand. He was actuated by another mind altogether, not the common religious mind of this earth, but the heavenly mind. Later when people did come to understand Him by revelation of the Holy Spirit, you have a big transformation. They were people who were not understood by this world, and yet what a heavenly kind of thing it was, how actuated by heavenly thoughts and conceptions, heavenly weights and measures, heavenly standards."
> T AUSTIN SPARKS

Heavenly standards. And children are seeing some of these realities ahead of us adults.
I heard a testimony of a little girl who received a visit one night from the Lord Jesus. I cannot imagine what they talked about but the next morning, a very excited little girl wanted to tell Mummy all about it. I paraphrase, not remembering her exact words, but they were along these lines:

"Mummy, all this (pointing around the room) is going. It's all just practice. Heaven is real. Do you see? This is all going to go."

How wonderful. This is no pipe dream.

I am secure in Christ. His presence and His approval is all that matters. Therefore I can make it my ambition to live out by grace perfecting holiness, not what I want to be but what I already am and who I will practically be for an eternity in heaven.

Randy Smith

8
THE LAMB'S BOOK OF LIFE

> " ...and nothing unclean, and no one who practices abomination and lying, shall ever come into it, but only those [ ]whose names are written in the Lamb's book of life."
> REVELATION 21:27

Assuming that the standards of Heaven's technology are light years ahead of even our most modern, digital enabling, I do wonder whether the Book in question is a traditional paper or parchment affair; or will we see administrative angels on their tablets and handheld devices? Whatever its format, this is a book that Revelation tells us will 'be opened". It is a faultless, comprehensive record of whatever Heaven deems to be important.

We read about it in our passage of Revelation but it also appears elsewhere. Bible scholars and commentators describe the prospects of there being more than a single book; in Revelation 13 we read of the 'book of life' which contains the names of those belonging to God since the foundation of the world. Is this the same book as described in Revelation 21?

Actually, I am not going to concern myself with the question. If my name appears in any of Jesus' books, signifying that I belong to Him, I am completely satisfied. I was once turned away from a West Ham football match, many years ago, having queued for some time. Those were the days when the line for entry into the North Bank standing area, behind one of the goals, would snake its way through the stadium's forecourts and gates into the parallel Green Street nearby.

On this occasion, I was in line with friends for a seat in the West Stand. I made it right to the turn style - a clanking claret, rotating entry mechanism, before being told that all tickets had now been sold. I could not get in.

A kind observer noticed what had happened and approached my group; he handed us some complimentary seats for which he no longer had use.

Genuine tickets – freely given – presumably paid for by him or a connection of his.

I vividly remember, to this day, seeing the price recorded on the ticket - £0.00. Someone had paid the ticket price on my behalf, assuring my entry. I had received the gift and was now part of the hordes of spectators, on an equal footing with everyone else. No matter that I had not paid a penny. The cost of entry had been borne.

The arena of Heaven will be occupied by those whose names are in the Lamb's Book of Life. Each and every one will bear the mark of belonging to Jesus. This is the real, genuine mark – the one obtained by receiving the Saviour, (Ephesians 1:13).

Revelation speaks of another mark – the Mark of the Beast. This mark will chain people to the ownership of the devil and his earthly associates forever. What a tragedy, what unspeakable horror for those who are going to find out what the reality of their decision to take this mark is. Having preferred an earthly outlook, they have ignored or not appreciated the eternal, spiritual consequences.

This is THE book that matters, over and above any work written by human hands. It is a book containing entries made by Heaven's representatives. Of course, we have the precious Bible – the written word of God – none of us would be in a position to even consider these spiritual matters and the person of Christ without it. In no way am I relegating the God breathed scriptures to any level less worthy than they deserve. The word of God stands forever.

> "For You have magnified Your [b]word [c]according to all Your name."
> PSALM 138:2

The opening of God's book(s) at a time of God's choosing, is surely a moment of which the significance cannot be overstated. Heaven will make an irreversible announcement concerning each person that has ever lived.

As a friend of Jesus Christ, your name is on the list. The administrative angel will not need to check twice. Your name will speak – it will witness to who you became when you accepted Jesus Christ into your life.

'UNKNOWN'

'Unknown' is a 2011 movie starring Liam Neeson. The entire plot is not relevant here but am I reminded of one, key scene.

Liam's character, Dr Martin Harris, arrives at a hotel in Berlin with his wife, Liz. He is due to take part in a conference that the hotel is hosting. They are checking in at the front desk when Martin remembers that he has left his briefcase on a baggage trolley at the airport. He will remedy it immediately and go collect it. He kisses his wife, goodbye.

Returning by taxi to retrieve the case, the car is involved in a road accident; Martin wakes up in hospital, apparently having been in a coma for four days. Nevertheless, he pretty much expects his affairs to continue as he recovers; he is, unsurprisingly, especially keen to find Liz.

He is concerned, at first, to learn that no-one – especially his wife - has enquired after him. He wonders why Liz has not been in contact with the authorities. He appears to have no identification to hand.

Discharging himself from hospital, Martin returns to the hotel and spots Liz in a downstairs lobby area. Mentioning his name to the hotel staff, he moves to pass through a counter to join her and many of the conference delegates who have gathered. He is stopped. He needs to show his id.

But he doesn't have any id. Becoming increasingly frustrated, he demands to be allowed to pass through into the conference area, having seen not only his wife but other colleagues, too, that he recognises. A hotel manager agrees to escort him to Liz and a relieved Dr Martin now expects this rather unwelcome misunderstanding to be swiftly concluded.

A nightmare moment ensues. Liz does not appear to recognise him. Not only that, but she introduces another man who she says is her husband, a Dr Martin Harris. Liam Neeson plays the incredulity of his character so well!

He just cannot compute what is going on. Imagine this was happening to you; how would you even begin to process this? Imagine the shock, the bewilderment, the desire to give everyone within five metres a hearty shake and declare, 'What's the matter with you all, it's me!'

Martin, despite his protests, is escorted away. No-one, there, knows who he is. His wife does not know who he is, and she is seen subsequently sitting down to a meal with her 'husband' in the hotel restaurant. Martin simply cannot be there because he cannot be identified. His name is not known and so he is not permitted to enter the venue.

One thing which will be true of our appearance at Heaven's 'counter' is that there will be no confusion. At least, not after an initial protest, perhaps.

> "[21]Not everyone who says to Me, 'Lord, Lord,' will enter the kingdom of heaven, but he who does the will of My Father who is in heaven *will enter*. [22] Many will say to Me on that day, 'Lord, Lord, did we not prophesy in Your name, and in Your name cast out demons, and in Your name perform many [a]miracles?' [23] And then I will declare to them, 'I never knew you; depart from Me, you who practice lawlessness.'
> MATTHEW 7: 21-23

When the Lord declares whether we are 'known' or 'unknown,' there will be no arguing. All will be in the light. God's justice will be plainly evident.

In Luke 10, the disciples cheerfully recount to the Lord their experiences of demonic authority giving way to the name of Jesus. But Jesus puts this in perspective and points them to something of greater significance.

> "[19]Behold, I have given you authority to tread on serpents and scorpions, and over all the power of the enemy, and nothing will injure you. [20] Nevertheless do not rejoice in this, that the spirits are subject to you, but rejoice that your names are recorded in heaven."
> Luke 10: 19-20

The deliverances and ministry are a vital outworking of the presence of the Kingdom among those who witness them; Jesus reminds his disciples that this work is a work of the Holy Spirit for His purposes and not something to focus on oneself with. We are encouraged that, 'Yes – you have authority in My name but using it is about establishing Kingdom freedom – it is for the Kingdom, not for some kind of personal measure.'

'But rejoice that your names are recorded in heaven.' I am delighted, thrilled that my name, Steve Hawkins, is recorded in Heaven. How about you? Is this real to you? Not only will you have access at Heaven's eternal counter, but you already belong and have access to the Father's house and all that He provides.

> "And he said to him, 'Son, you [m]have always been with me, and all that is mine is yours…'"
> LUKE 15:31

In Luke 15, the father in the parable addresses his elder son's faulty mindset. He just had not imagined or considered the generosity of his father and was, therefore, surprised and offended when he witnessed the outpouring of grace for his younger brother.

As sons and daughters of the House, may we fully participate in our adoption and status has family members. Hebrews 4 speaks of our coming to the throne of grace with confidence; our confidence is in the perfect Son. We can afford to be generous towards each other, just as our heavenly Father shows us grace, mercy and abundance.

It is time to settle into the business of being part of the household of Heaven. Prayer, worship, relationship, Kingdom influence – let us fully engage with God as He directs us.

9
AMBASSADORS

> "¹⁶Therefore from now on we recognize no one [l]according to the flesh; even though we have known Christ [g]according to the flesh, yet now we know *Him in this way* no longer. ¹⁷ Therefore if anyone is in Christ, [h]*he is* a new creature; the old things passed away; behold, new things have come. ¹⁸ Now all *these* things are from God, who reconciled us to Himself through Christ and gave us the ministry of reconciliation, ¹⁹ namely, that God was in Christ reconciling the world to Himself, not counting their trespasses against them, and [l]He has [l]committed to us the word of reconciliation. ²⁰ Therefore, we are ambassadors for Christ, as though God were making an appeal through us; we beg you on behalf of Christ, be reconciled to God. ²¹ He made Him who knew no sin *to be* sin on our behalf, so that we might become the righteousness of God in Him."
> 2 CORINTHIANS 5: 16-21

The verses above summarise the Good News beautifully and also establish a key role for Christian believers in these days.

Paul encourages us to understand that as we now relate to Jesus as the glorified King of Kings, so we relate to those around us from that perspective. The Church has been set a mission and Jesus promises to be in step with us at every point along the way.

Through His finished work on the Cross, we engage with those around us as ambassadors. Just as we have aligned ourselves to this work, received the Spirit and become children of God, so we are to see others around us in terms of their Kingdom status and belonging.

They will only belong to the Kingdom through Christ, as do we.

In a later chapter we are going to look at the roles and ministries that God has gifted to the Church; for now, let us acknowledge that although the gifting of evangelists to the world is a key provision, not all of us are called to blossom in the same manner in that gifting.

> But – we are all expected to "do the work of an evangelist," (2 Timothy 4)

Many believers seem to struggle with sharing their faith. Is it the fear of man, wanting a 'way' or 'format' to speak to others? Perhaps we simply believe we are 'too busy.' I think, however, that my forty plus years of walking with Jesus have shown me something to simplify the matter. Do I have something to say, or not? If so, what?

This stance has really helped me. Whilst admiring the passion, precision and focus of those more evangelistically minded than I am, I've also come to realise that I have a unique testimony which doesn't necessarily sit well among this or that method of communicating with people. Do I have something to say? Absolutely. I understand the key, gospel truths and I -we-surely can put those into words for others. Because it matters, doesn't it?

As we have seen in the last chapter, only those whose names are written in the Lamb's Book of Life will join us in Heaven's stunning, new society. Do we believe that? God, in Christ, was reconciling the world to Himself, we have read, and we have been given the ministry of enabling that reconciliation for those who cross into our sphere of influence.

Not every church body may employ an evangelist or be able to say – yes – 'he' or 'she' is our principal evangelist. But every church body is packed with ambassadors.

It's in your salvation pack. Check the tote bag that you were issued with when you became part of Heaven's family. Paul states that he has become an ambassador, appealing to those he meets and to those who read his letters, to be reconciled to God (2 Corinthians 5).

Being reconciled to God is everything, when you think about it. People need to know that even they were to gain all that the world can offer, it will be worth nothing at all compared to knowing Jesus Christ (Mark 8).

We have dealt with the issue of whether we are worthy enough, qualified enough, to speak for the Lord. That qualification was never about our own efforts and still is not today. Christ has qualified and appointed us.

Becoming the righteousness of God is everything because without it, no-one will see the Life of Heaven.

SCENT OR STINK?

> "14But thanks be to God, who always leads us in triumph in Christ, and manifests through us the sweet aroma of the knowledge of Him in every place. 15 For we are a fragrance of Christ to God among those who are being saved and among those who are perishing; 16 to the one an aroma from death to death, to the other an aroma from life to life."
> 2 CORINTHIANS 2: 14-16

The message of the Kingdom is a sweet aroma. Many will discern that sweetness and taste the Life of Christ contained within it. Other will not; their self-centred stance and refusal to acknowledge the truth of who Jesus is will determine their experience of the gospel – 'death.' They are in spiritual death, now, and wish to remain so. They are deciding to pass on God's grace and continue in their current, spiritual state of separation from God.
They are ignoring the pleas and invitations of the ambassadors.
Nevertheless, the ambassadors are unfazed. They will continue to represent the interests of the domain from which they have been appointed and sent. That is what ambassadors do. They know who they are and *whose* they are. They understand that the authority that they carry has been delegated to them and entrusted to them. Ambassadors are officials of the highest rank.

That's right. We regularly hear of and are encouraged by our need to trust God. To trust Him with all our heart. But how about this? God trusts you and me.

We are trusted to exercise the ambassadorial role to the Kingdom of Heaven and the kingdom of darkness. We act for the Kingdom's interests and home *and abroad.*

Much of the time, we are very tangibly 'abroad.' We may be living among broken people, torn families, individuals who are masking serious illness through their addictions and behaviours. We may work within organisations that are dishonest and arm themselves with deeds of darkness in order to seek to get ahead.

Such people do not know, in all probability, that there is a father who is waiting for them to turn to Him. We know, from the Bible account, with what passion and abandon the father runs to his lost, younger son when he sees him on the horizon. May the Holy Spirit clothe us with that same desire to embrace others.

Let us recall the basis upon which we know that, as ambassadors, we hold the delegated authority of the Kingdom of Heaven.

> "And He said to them, "I was watching Satan fall from heaven like lightning…"
> LUKE 10:18

The rebellious angel has been cast down and his influence, appalling as it is, is a temporary one. His kingdom is doomed to destruction. As ambassadors, we get to see moments where darkness is overcome, where captives discover freedom in Jesus and where evil strongholds are shifted.

"Religion says earn your life. Secular society says create your life. Jesus says, 'My life for your life'."

Timothy Keller

10
BLOOD – UNDERSTOOD IN HEAVENLY PLACES

The first murder to take place on planet Earth saw Abel killed by his brother, Cain. In Genesis 4, the Lord announces that the blood of this man "cries out" to Him from the ground where Abel has fallen. The blood is speaking.

In Hebrews, we are reminded that our names have been logged – we have been enrolled into the Kingdom. It is by the blood of Jesus Christ that our covenant stands and will stand for all eternity.

> "22 But you have come to Mount Zion and to the city of the living God, the heavenly Jerusalem, and to myriads of [b]angels, 23 to the general assembly and church of the firstborn who are enrolled in heaven, and to God, the Judge of all, and to the spirits of *the* righteous made perfect, 24 and to Jesus, the mediator of a new covenant, and to the sprinkled blood, which speaks better than *the blood* of Abel."
> HEBREWS 12: 22-24

The blood of Christ announces to all realms that reconciliation, relationship and authority have been restored and that men may now freely approach the Father, having been redeemed by the Son. The children of the Kingdom may approach the Father of the Kingdom. The children have become family because each one has received the work of the Cross as a personal transaction.

I seem to remember a criticism of a particular Bible translation, many years ago. The word 'blood' was translated as 'death' and – yes – it is all about the death and resurrection of the Son of God. But as unpleasant and as raw it is to consider the shedding of blood, to do so is to more certainly grasp what was at stake when Jesus went to the Cross.

Our identity is entirely soaked – covered – filled with the blood of Jesus. There is simply no getting away from it. It is what separates Christianity as a faith from any other so-called faith, philosophy or religion.

Not that such religions do not deal in blood. They do – *and they do so because the power of blood is understood in the heavenly realms.* The shedding of blood in any religious ceremony is an attempt to placate or please a deity of some description. But there is only one blood that counts. Only one is relevant. The others are shadows, substitutes to the true, divine blood that achieves the goal of Heaven.

We have been saved for purpose – the goal is to give God pleasure and to partner with Him in His dealings with mankind. We must be sure of the significance of the blood of Jesus.

HISTORY HINTS

The history of the Jewish people points to the coming Messiah – many scriptures in the Psalms and Isaiah, for example, reveal Him; the heavenly realms have always known that Jesus Christ would need to be born, grow up, minister as a man on earth, be crucified and then rise again from the dead.

Satan systematically tried to destroy Jesus and to prevent this entire Kingdom work from being successful. You can imagine some kind of banner across the gates of hell as a constant reminder to demonic forces: JESUS CHRIST MUST NOT BE ALLOWED TO DECLARE, "IT IS FINISHED!"

And so with the prophetic hope of a new born Saviour, Herod, under Satan's guidance, attempts to wipe out every male child. Satan had practised this kind of appalling operation before, attempting to murder every male infant in an effort to prevent the ministry of Moses.

Prophetic dreams to Joseph and to the so-called 'wise men' ensure that Herod's plans are thwarted. How we need to respect and honour the Kingdom gift of prophetic ministry and dreams!

There are plots and attempts to kill Jesus during His ministry. On one occasion, having read from the Torah and declared that He is the fulfilment of scripture in Isaiah, the enraged listeners march Him out of the meeting place to the brow of a hill with the intention of murdering Him.

> "[21]And He closed the [a]book, gave it back to the attendant and sat down; and the eyes of all in the synagogue were fixed on Him. [22] And He began to say to them, "Today this Scripture has been fulfilled in your [b]hearing."... [28] And all *the people* in the synagogue were filled with rage as they heard these things; [29] and they got up and drove Him out of the city, and led Him to the brow of the hill on which their city had been built, in order to throw Him down the cliff. [30] But passing through their midst, He went His way."
> LUKE 4: 21-22, 28-30

The authority of the Son of God said, 'No.' No – it is not going to happen this way. It is written how it will happen but this is not it. It is not the time, nor the place, nor the way.

> "[14] Just as Moses lifted up the snake in the wilderness, so the Son of Man must be lifted up,[a] [15] that everyone who believes may have eternal life in him."
> JOHN 3:14

And

> "[31] For He was teaching His disciples and telling them, "The Son of Man is to be [a]delivered into the hands of men, and they will kill Him; and when He has been killed, He will rise three days later."
> MARK 9:31

History shows us that since time immemorial, men have shed blood as a means of trying to obtain spiritual power, to appease 'gods' or to seek their favour. It still happens today; the following describes Islam's Eid un Adha celebration:

"The streets of Dhaka are ready to run with blood. It can only mean one thing – Eid ul Adha, Islam's annual festival of sacrifice is here....."

"Hundreds of thousands of cattle will be sacrificed in the capital and across Bangladesh …. most animals will be slaughtered in the street, leaving the stench of blood hanging in the air for days …"
BBC, 2004

Other Islamic festivals also deal in the currency of blood; at the time of Ashura, Shiite pilgrims indulge in a bloody self-flagellation, using sharp objects such as swords, razors and knives.

Hinduism involves sacrifice and the shedding of blood: Raksha Bandhan is a celebration held to honour the relationship between brothers and sisters; a two-day party has worshippers gathering at shrines and animal sacrifices are made; hundreds of bulls and goats may be killed and the people mark their foreheads with the blood.

Did you hear that? *The people mark their foreheads with the blood.* This is about ownership – belonging – a price paid; it is a spiritual act, one designed to control and manipulate. The individual invests their faith in these acts, believes that there is benefit and that the supernatural realm is an ally.

Do you know, Christian, that you have a mark on your head *already*? God has sealed you into Christ Jesus.

> "[13] In [c]Him, you also, after listening to the message of truth, the gospel of your salvation—having also [d]believed, you were sealed in [e]Him with the Holy Spirit of promise, [14] who is [f]given as a pledge of our inheritance, with a view to the redemption of *God's own* possession, to the praise of His glory."
> EPHESIANS 1: 13-14

Revelation 7 speaks of a time in the future when the Lord will pour out judgements on the earth – but not until "we have sealed the bondservants of our God on their foreheads."

A seal is an 'emblem of authentication' according to one definition. In Him we have been authentically sealed as people of His Kingdom and from this place of glorious acceptance and love, we live in His name, for His name.

THE PASSION OF THE CHRIST

Mel Gibson's controversial portrayal of the shedding of Jesus' blood drew much attention when his movie was released around the world in 2004. We do baulk at the shedding of blood. Even some of our medical professionals struggle with the sight of it.

There is something – what is the word – *sacred* about blood? We know that without it, we die. We know that when it ceases flowing around our bodies, we stop functioning. If blood matters so enormously in the earthly, temporal realm, can we imagine how significant it is in the spiritual realm?

As a Christian, you are a dangerous character in the heavenly realms – dangerous to demons and a delight to the Kingdom of Light. The unique, sinless, perfect Blood from Jesus Christ has fashioned you into an eternal citizen of Heaven.

Still, there are believers who feel awkward around the subject of Jesus' crucifixion; perhaps it is a sense of awe, a sense of debt, a sense of gratitude that cannot be put into words. As ambassadors, I do think there is a time and place to do just that – to try to put Jesus' suffering into words. Because it was a completely unique event.

"One of the world's leading authorities on the subject, Professor John Granger Cook of LaGrange College, Georgia, US, estimates that between around 200BC and the virtual abolition of crucifixion in AD337, between 100,000 and 150,000 people were crucified in Roman-controlled territories."
THE INDEPENDENT, DECEMBER 2001

It is known that victims were thoroughly flogged before their ordeal of the crossed beams; some would not even make it to their final execution site. Jewish law restricted a beating to forty lashes, and thirty-nine would be counted out to ensure that the limit was not exceeded. There were no such restrictions in Roman punishment.

In response to criticism that the scenes of Jesus' whipping in the movie were unnecessarily graphic and exaggerated, Gibson responded with the admission that the scenes were probably unrealistic – in that they were not graphic enough. Is it all just too long ago? Does the space in time some diminish the impact of what were truly gruesome, torturous executions?

The Independent article quoted from above includes an unpleasant photograph of a relic from Roman Cambridgeshire, namely an excavated heel bone with a nail driven through it. Crucifixion was clearly practised in Roman Britain.

Jesus Christ was flogged as part of his pre-crucifixion punishment. If you are interested, you can find several videos online in which qualified and learned commentators explain the medical ramifications of such an ordeal.

The Bible shows the physical damage to Jesus in Isaiah's prophecy. There is a simple statement which, if digested, makes painful reading.

"So His appearance was marred beyond *that of a* man, And His form beyond the sons of mankind."

> "Many people were shocked when they saw him. His appearance was so damaged he did not look like a man; his form was so changed they could barely tell he was human" -
> The New Century Version
> ISAIAH 52:14

I have no desire to upset you and I hope you see that I am not focusing here on Jesus' suffering from a gratuitous motive. Blood matters. At the Temple in Jerusalem, there were occasions when, literally, uncountable numbers of animals were sacrificed; blood flowed freely.

So when you and I step out into our day, identified with the sinless Blood of Christ, we should be deliberate about using our delegated authority. Our words can bring life, healing, conviction and comfort. We may see others through the lens of Kingdom people, esteeming our brothers and sisters in Christ and being open to what the Lord may have us express to those who have not met Him yet.

Only by identifying with His blood will *anyone* cross into eternal life. It's a message in need of declaration to all who will hear it.

"If our identity is in our work, rather than Christ, success will go to our heads, and failure will go to our hearts."

Timothy Keller

11
MOTIVES

"¹⁹ Therefore Jesus answered and was saying to them, "Truly, truly, I say to you, the Son can do nothing of Himself, unless *it is* something He sees the Father doing; for whatever [ᵃ]the Father does, these things the Son also does in like manner."

> "Jesus told the people: I tell you for certain the Son cannot do anything on his own. He can do only what he sees the Father doing, and he does exactly what he sees the Father do" -The Contemporary English Version
> JOHN 5:19

Paul encourages believers in this way.

> "¹⁶ But I say, walk by the Spirit, and you will not carry out the desire of the flesh. ¹⁷ For the flesh [ᵃ]sets its desire against the Spirit, and the Spirit against the flesh; for these are in opposition to one another, so that you may not do the things that you [ᵇ]please. ¹⁸ But if you are led by the Spirit, you are not under the Law."
> GALATIANS 5: 16-18

In these days the Church needs to listen to Jesus Christ. We are still sheep, however clever, learned and advanced we think we may have become. Sheep need their shepherd; Christians need to heed the Shepherd. The Shepherd will never allow us to become independent of Him, of our need to hear and follow His voice. He will not permit the Church to function effectively *apart from Him.*

Do many churches appear to 'function' apart from him? Well, yes. Those attending gatherings of such churches seem to know exactly what is going to happen each time they meet; the structure is set; it has all been meticulously planned. I have to wonder to what degree such meetings are *about* the Lord rather than them being times *of* the Lord. Does He take centre stage or is He a frustrated observer?

The world must see that only God is its hope. Not even a beautifully managed Church will be able to achieve even the smallest measure of Kingdom effectiveness unless God is in the midst.

Jesus modelled this perfectly for us. During His earthly life, He lived a heavenly life. He always committed Himself to a living awareness of what His Father was doing and aligned Himself to that. Because He knew that this would be effective *every time*.
Onlookers may make their judgements and suggest that He could have done more or might have done less.

Jesus was not interested in the opinions of those only too ready to give their view. Jesus' vision was steadfastly set on His Father's will and pleasure.

> "[28] So Jesus said, "When you lift up the Son of Man, then you will know that [a]I am *He*, and I do nothing on My own initiative, but I speak these things as the Father taught Me. [29] And He who sent Me is with Me; He [b]has not left Me alone, for I always do the things that are pleasing to Him." [30] As He spoke these things, many came to believe in Him."
> JOHN 8: 28-30

The fruit of the Lord's determination to please the Father is that 'many came to believe in Him.' Isn't that exactly what we want, too? What, really, are our motives?

The Kingdom of God is upside down in terms of the world's values and desire to please. In many respects, the world wants to please people so that it can gain their allegiance. I am always impacted – and disappointed – when I hear failing political parties announce that they need to change course and 'give the people what they want'.

This is not leadership. This is some form of twisted bribery. 'People didn't like our last manifesto, so we'll change it all around, perhaps stand for the opposite point of view, and then, maybe, we will attract more votes.'

Leadership is about desiring to serve others with what is right.

The verses above from John 8 illustrate an absolutely trustworthy Saviour who has set his face to follow and please His Father above all others. He is unflinching. Whatever the test, whatever the opposition, He has already decided upon His direction.

He has the constant assurance that He is not 'left alone'. His Father is backing Him without fail.

SUCCESS

A successful church body is one that fulfils the mandate to which God has called it. That charge may be a little – or seem very – different to a neighbouring church group.

The measure of success is not the size of our congregation, the make-up of our worship band or the A-list of speakers that may visit our meetings. It will not be the quality of our tea and coffee, although the provision of chocolate Bourbon biscuits surely is worthy of note in the Kingdom ...

'We are upgrading our sanctuary!' Lovely. Why? Is this decision following a leading from the Lord? Is that what He is showing the church to do? Otherwise, what is the point?

All churches will have elements in common. They are set up to be families, because God builds through family and through relationships. They will be people of prayer and worship because that is what believers do – our life response to our God is to pray, to seek Him, to love Him, to worship Him.

Above all, a church needs to be a people of His Presence. It is the dynamic, Emmanuel presence of the Holy Spirit that makes all the difference. I remember attending a large, Christian rally on one occasion. There were thousands of people. As a time of praise loudly preceded the messages that would follow, I became very aware of *the lack of anointing* in that place.

Conversely, I imagine that many of you can relate to being present at the smallest of gatherings in which the invited Lord beautifully touched lives in a time of unique intimacy.

I am not saying that all large gatherings lack the power of God. By no means. But if the Spirit of God is not allowed freedom to move among the church, we may as well admit that we are just playing church. Should you visit the church family I am part of, I hope that the key memory to stay with you will be the way in which His presence touched your life.

I can promise you this – if you were to ask me in advance about the meeting you are to attend, I would be able to tell you very little. Unless He chooses to speak to us in advance, I have no idea, really, what God is going to do. I don't know how long the meeting will last, I don't know who may share during our time of praise and worship, I don't know who will see visions or receive words of knowledge. I *do* know that we will invite the Lord to move in whatever way He pleases.

Increasingly, we realise that it is *He* who invites *us* to share in what He is doing. We are also growing in our recognition that our worship of the Lord is a lifestyle. May His anointing be in our car journeys, in our workplaces, at the supermarket, in the garden, in a restaurant, perhaps.

Our security in our Kingdom identity will determine the degree to which we are genuinely living for the purpose of His glory; walking in step with the Lord, acting and speaking as we perceive the Father is acting and speaking.

In other words, expecting to see 'on earth as it is in Heaven.' For years many of us have sung: 'We wanna see Jesus lifted high! A banner that flies across this land.' Our greatest freedom, our greatest thrill and our grandest achievement are to see the name of Jesus Christ honoured within our sphere of influence and throughout the land.

May our lives, our homes, our churches and the places where we live become 'thin places' where others can discern and be impacted by the presence of the Lord. In such environments, there is no room for a competitive spirit and the insecurity that shows itself through boasting, self-justification and that needy requirement that everyone should know about the part that *I* have been playing. We might not want to admit it, but we are only revealing our lack of understanding as to who we really are as sons and daughters of the House.

We are all very different and have walked unique paths to get to where we are now, in the Lord. Comparing ourselves with others is fairly ridiculous. We are far too multi-faceted. For many years, I knew that in some aspects of my faith walk, I lacked maturity; while in others, I was progressing well.

We are all going to meet men, women and children who, to some degree appear to be behind us in terms of elements of our Christian Walk; equally, we will meet many who are ahead – or appear to streak ahead before our eyes!

If Jesus is being glorified, we should celebrate their expressions of Him! Comparing ourselves with others is usually a fairly fruitless exercise, unless we are spurred on positively and healthily by what the Lord is doing in their lives.

In the New Testament, Paul encourages Timothy to press into Jesus and not be concerned about his age – he may have been a 16–20-year-old when he first came on the scene around Paul's ministry.

But there are children considerably younger than that who know the Lord, listen to His voice and speak on His behalf. Scripture reminds us how we should see them – indeed – everyone in the Body of Christ.

In 2 Corinthians 5, Paul reminds us that our earthly body is merely a temporary dwelling place for our spirit man – that we have a heavenly dwelling place in the eternal realm. What is mortal will, one day, be 'swallowed up' by life – our full, eternal being will supersede our current, flesh and blood bodies. The Holy Spirit's presence in our life is a 'pledge,' – a guarantee of what is to come.

This applies to all of us; we are created in the image of God and have been born again in Christ Jesus; we are to see each and honour one another in the light of our new identity.

> "16 Therefore from now on we recognize no one [1]according to the flesh; even though we have known Christ [2]according to the flesh, yet now we know *Him in this way* no longer. 17 Therefore if anyone is in Christ, [3]*he is* a new

creature; the old things passed away; behold, new things have come."
2 CORINTHIANS 5: 17-18

Take a closer look at your Christian family. These are Kingdom people; people who were lost and have now been found; people who are no longer of the earthly realm but are seated in Heaven with Christ Jesus; they are new creations, and the life of Christ is now working within and through them to bring God pleasure and to transform them into the likeness of the Son. What a miracle they are!

One day you will see them – and they will see you – in unadulterated glory. The whole truth of you will be evident and we will recognise that we are all trophies of His grace.

May the motivations of our hearts stay on track; as we worship the Lord through our lives in their various expressions and as we pray for the fame of Heaven to be established, His favour will surround us, promote us and ensure that the name, love and works of Jesus Christ are what those around us and our churches note us for.

"Christian maturity requires that we ask whether we are more motivated by gratitude for God's mercy or by a futile attempt to earn it."

Bryan Chapell

12
FIVE REASONS TO YIELD

In these few pages, we have covered some important ground. Recognizing our place within the five-fold ministry of the Church will enable us to truly delight in the shape and purpose of our lives as part of the Body of Christ.

Jesus says that His 'yoke' is easy and that his burden is light. Picture the oxen yoked together before the plow, needing to walk together, sharing the weight of the task. As long as the oxen keep course, the yoke upon their necks will be 'easy.' There is one direction for them to walk in, and one only.

I struggle a little with the often-spoken idea that God 'uses' us. Perhaps it is the modern connotation of 'using' that bothers me; the notion that someone's attributes, talents or possessions are the focus of another's interest more than the person themselves. A relationship issue may prompt a concerned observer to comment, 'He's just using her...' Perhaps an employment difficulty stems from a supervisor taking advantage of a team member's talents rather than having the person's interests at heart.

Of course, the Lord *does* use us and we want to be fruitful for Him. But the care with which he treats us, values us and loves us render the term 'use' almost inappropriate by today's standards.

Beautifully, you might argue that there are as many expressions of Christian ministry as there are believers! We are unique, we know that. We have each been crafted by the Creator. None of us could possibly fit into the box assigned us by another human being – how could they know us well enough to do so? But our Father has fashioned us to wear His yoke comfortably and profitably.

Many believers seem to struggle to find their place or position in their church body. The fault is not with the Lord. Something needs to change with us. Are we trying to force ourselves to take on a particular shape to fit someone else's expectation?

Among the billions who profess the name of the Lord, the Bible points to five principal areas of ministry that God has gifted to the Church; the aim is that the Church grows up, maturing into constancy and a solid walk with God.

A church should not enter crisis because the principal leader or leaders is/are away for several days. A mature body will continue to operate as each one moves in the manner to which the Lord has fashioned them.

In Ephesians 4, Paul reminds us that we are all part of one Body. There will only ever be one. This truth will make the largest congregation appreciate just how tiny they are; moreover, it will encourage the smallest of faithful gatherings that they are wonderfully vital in the overall Body of Christ.

> "4 *There is* one body and one Spirit, just as also you were called in one hope of your calling; 5 one Lord, one faith, one baptism, 6 one God and Father of all who is over all and through all and in all."
> EPHESIANS 4: 4-6

And now the description of this divine provision:

> "11 And He gave some *as* apostles, and some *as* prophets, and some *as* evangelists, and some *as* pastors and teachers,12 for the equipping of the [i]saints for the work of service, to the building up of the body of Christ; 13 until we all attain to the unity of the faith, and of the [j]knowledge of the Son of God, to a mature man, to the measure of the stature [i]which belongs to the fullness of Christ. 14 [j]As a result, we are no longer to be children, tossed here and there by waves and carried about by every wind of doctrine, by the trickery of men, by craftiness [h]in deceitful scheming; 15 but [i]speaking the truth in love, [j]we are to grow up in all *aspects* into Him who is the head, *even* Christ, 16 from whom the whole body, being fitted and held together [k]by what every joint supplies, according to the [l]proper working of each individual part, causes the growth of the body for the building up of itself in love."

Let us note that the fruit of this ministry is unity. I mean – real unity. I am not talking about the occasional meeting together of various churches. I am not referring to man sparked initiatives to provoke a sense of togetherness. I mean – the real thing *from Heaven's standpoint.*

Unity is the Church functioning according to Heaven's mandate. You *know* when there is Holy Spirit unity between believers or groups of believers; there is an ease, there is joy, there is peace and an absence of striving or competition.

The 'other' is preferred and there is delight in supporting and furthering their goals. It is evident that in preferring them, you, yourselves, are strengthened. It would be a profitable thing to pray that more churches find, or locate, other groups of believers that the Lord would have them network with.

We may be surprised at what that looks like. The maturing of the Church according to Ephesians 4 will enable her to grow up – to 'no longer be children.' Adults are seasoned people – they have proven the substance and reality of the word of God in life experience. They have become – or at least are becoming – people who are solid in God whatever their personal circumstances or wider issues of the nation might throw at them. They are at peace with themselves and the Lord – they have matured to a place of *rest.*

I highly recommend Dan Stone's, 'The Rest of the Gospel' (2000, One Press), which explains very clearly how Christian maturity releases us from striving so that the life of Christ may be free to express itself (Himself!) through our lives.

People of character hold their ground in a crisis. They show leadership. They show in Whom they have put their trust. They don't throw their hands up in the air declaring doom. There is no doom in the Kingdom of God. To seek the Lord is a reflex for them because they live like that anyway as a matter of course.

They do not draw on God only when there is trouble; they do so because the Christian life is about drawing on God at all times. How can we live to "only do what we see the Father doing" if our eyes are not trained upon Him *as a matter of course?*

Every joint is to supply the Body. I'm sure you've heard some amusing anecdotes from friends of yours. 'Oh, I'm only a thumb in the Body' or, 'He *must* be a mouth!' You might even have heard someone preach about the vital role of the thumb in biology! It is a crucial appendage, actually!

Christ is the head, Ephesians teaches us; we are growing up into Him. We are part of Him. Gloriously, Christ now lives in us, and we live in Him. He has fused us to Himself in the substance of His blood.

I think that we may misunderstand the five-fold ministry of apostles, prophets, evangelists, pastors and teachers. Certainly, if we perceive the list to be in an order of merit or status in a local church.

I do believe that there are prophetic ministries which hold an authority not just in a single church but in many. Such prophetic ministries can be of tremendous support and encouragement to regions and even across international borders. All these borders are earthly things; they are not relevant in the same way in the spiritual, heavenly realm.

Additionally, apostolic ministries can marvellously strengthen and help support the planting and establishment of churches over a wide domain. It is unlikely that every local church is going to have a highly influential person of every gifting.

As far as our local churches are concerned, the ministries are likely to be different but can clearly complement one another. It is not so much a top-down list as a pie chart. Christ is the Head; the ministries work through the Body to cause growth. Generally, a leadership team is likely to be headed up by men and women with pastoral giftings, but pastors may not necessarily be the overall church leaders.

What really counts is that the team works together in the love of Christ and desires, above all, that the Lord has His way in and through the body they are part of. An important side to this will be recognising and praying into the giftings and growth of their congregation; instilling godly character will be prioritised over giftings, but the latter should be encouraged to flourish and given space to do so.

Churches are families; that's the plan. I believe that the Lord calls us to and plants us in a church body. We need that accountability. We need to be accountable to one another and to godly, compassionate leadership.

You should not really be able to 'hide' in a church. Yes, there are very large churches where many people seem to attend on a weekly basis without ever truly developing relational links with others. I am sure that through house groups and similar set-ups, the case is different elsewhere.

Smaller churches can be more closely knit in terms of the relationships enjoyed by its people; I've heard the complaint that it can feel a little like being in a goldfish bowl but – hey – if people are caring for you and looking out for you, that has to be a good thing.

We need to respect boundaries, too. Some issues are just not anyone else's business. We need to discern the intimacy levels that are appropriate for our various, church contacts and friends.

I want to encourage us to see that God has a fruitful place for us in the body in which He plants us. If we continually feel frustrated or tense, something isn't right. Frustration and tension do not speak of an 'easy yolk'. Why are we unsettled?

Perhaps we need to talk it out with a trusted leader or friend. It can be that our own attitude needs aligning – do we need to repent of a bad attitude? Are we holding unforgiveness against someone or is there a buried hurt that is triggering us emotionally? Or, perhaps, we are feeling boxed in, somehow unable to really express who we are at this place in our spiritual walk.

When the Lord is working in our lives, there are times and seasons; the wisdom of those around us can help us steer a biblical and Spirit-led way through difficult and uncertain times.

I am sure of this; if the Lord has planted us in a church body, then we should embrace that placement with all of our hearts; every church hits rough seas together with the charged moments and times of refreshing and blessing but I would not decide to leave a church unless the Lord was making it very plain to me – and also was confirming it to my leadership.

The Lord has placed giftings in your life and qualities that will enable you to fulfil 'the Maker's Instructions.' Helpful and trusted leaders will not be fazed by your growth but will be championing you, urging you forward and encouraging you to share with others those aspects of the Christian Walk that you have grown to be trusted in.

All of us have been allocated the ministry of reconciliation; what a huge honour.

> "[18] Now all *these* things are from God, who reconciled us to Himself through Christ and gave us the ministry of reconciliation, [19] namely, that God was in Christ reconciling the world to Himself, not counting their trespasses against them, and []He has []committed to us the word of reconciliation. [20] Therefore, we are ambassadors for Christ, as though God were making an appeal through us; we beg you on behalf of Christ, be reconciled to God."
> 2 CORINTHIANS 5: 18-20

With that, you will be aware of areas of supporting the Body of Christ which are particularly important to you – or – perhaps – others have told you that you are effective in them. You are a natural in embracing those who are new in the faith; you carry a burden for those who are within your sphere of influence who have not yet come to faith in Christ; you find yourself aware of impressions or knowledge of others' situations that only the Spirit of God could possibly have shown you; you have wisdom to deal with issues in the work place and suggest godly solutions that supervisors find helpful. Meeting other shoppers in the supermarket, it seems easy for you to open conversations that invariably lead to your sharing Jesus with them.

Perhaps you are part of the family's throng who have walked some bitter roads; along such ways you discovered the reality of Emmanuel – God with us – you experienced His comfort, His rescue, His many interventions. The tears that you have cried have qualified you as a bearer of others' pains and you find that your shoulders are, now, often damp with the tears of your brothers or sisters.

Or is it the case that as a reader of the word you seem to have a knack for explaining God's heart in the scriptures in ways that others can readily grasp.

As you minister from the Bible, a lot more than head knowledge is enhanced; hearts are touched as the Holy Spirit downloads revelation to your listeners. You may not even remember certain comments that you made but spiritual ears heard you and hearts have been strengthened.

Maybe you are aware that like-minded contacts have been springing up around you, recently. You are able to help these believers, and their leaders strategize ways forward and support them as they seek to put into practice the plans that the Lord has been revealing to them. Were someone to ask you *how* such relationships had sprung into your sphere of influence, you probably wouldn't know how to answer. God has been at work – that you do know.

These latter paragraphs, I hope, will encourage you that God has His ways of showing us how we fit into His body and into His Kingdom plans. The proof really is in the pudding. I have never wanted to label myself, particularly. But enough observers have recognised that I prophesy with accuracy and – am often shown the Lord's heart for His wider Church. I have also found that as I lead worship on the keyboard, people enter the presence of the Lord and He moves in their lives.

I don't really need the label or a badge. I will aim to fulfil my part in the Body and leave the rest to Him. God has fashioned each of us uniquely and, to His design and purpose, we fit into Kingdom ministry. I hope, rather than being burdened by question marks, that we will consider it an adventure to ascertain and enjoy the part(s) that God has for us.

When we are confident in our identity in Christ, then our true selves ~ our God-given personalities, gifts, and passions ~ can shine bright.

www.theoverflowing.com

13
DAILY REST

Rest is the soil in which we grow as Christians and from which we minister His life.

> "…but the people who know their God will display strength and take action."
>
> "…but the people that know their God shall be strong, and do *exploits*. " - American Standard Version
> DANIEL 11:32

We have covered a lot of ground, I hope you will agree on the subject of our identity in Jesus Christ in the pages thus far.

We have come to know the Lord by the power of the Holy Spirit and His revelation; we have come to the Father through the Son. We have 'been seated', according to Ephesians, in the heavenly places with Jesus Christ. We have seen that the victorious ones 'sit'. We sit because the battle is over – the work has been finished. It is finished for us because we have allied ourselves to Jesus' work upon the Cross in which He proclaimed, 'It is finished.'

Yes, there is still a fight. Yes, there are enemies yet to be trodden under His feet. Yes, we will face opposition and the demonic realm and the consequences of living in a sin-infested environment.

But we will never be alone. He has promised never to leave us or forsake us. How could He forsake us? He, who gave His life for us and considered the horrors that He underwent as 'joy', knowing that we, among millions, would be the enduring, precious fruit of His sufferings.

Unless we live from a place of rest, we shall not carry the weight of Kingdom exploits. To do His works means that we must refrain from doing our own.

To walk in the comfort of His yoke, we must be yoked only to Him and not to other agendas, however enticing or churchy they may appear to be.

Those of us who live in rest will fear only Him. To 'fear' here means to have the highest regard. In this way we will not be distracted by trying to please people or to meet their expectations. Perhaps they have already decided, in their own minds, how you are going to support them or what role you are going to play. If it isn't God's expression of who you are, there will only be frustration. You will not be living in divine rest.

SABBATH LIFE

The Jews were required to observe the Sabbath, 'Shabbat', they call it. Exodus 21 declares the weekly stipulation. God promised His people that they would profit more from working six days, honouring Shabbat, than if they worked for an income over seven days.

It's simple really. God blesses His word and blesses those who abide by it. The maths might suggest that you would earn more from an extra day's efforts; with God, however, there is a supernatural order of blessing which is not dependent upon reasoning and such calculations.

The Jewish Sabbath is a weekly celebration and, of all aspects of Jewish life, plays a hugely prominent part in the psyche. There are different streams of Jewish practice, from the strict Orthodox traditions to the Liberal and Reform synagogues. What they especially share, however, is the love of the Sabbath.

The Sabbath is evidence of belonging to God. How's that for an identity boost? The Jews know that they are marked out as His possession and that He – God – the God of Abraham, Isaac and Jacob – commanded respect for and adherence to the Rest Day.

Rest says, 'I belong'.

Only the Jewish tradition truly knows the meaning of the term 'shalom' which is loosely translated as 'peace.' Shalom is much more than that; shalom is a deep, abiding sense of well-being. Shalom says that we are completely secure in our belonging to God.

The New Testament tells Christians that the Sabbath, with many of the traditions and celebrations of Judaism, is a shadow of the reality that we have in Jesus Christ.

> "⁹So there remains a Sabbath rest for the people of God. ¹⁰ For the one who has entered His rest has himself also rested from his works, as God did from His. ¹¹ Therefore let us be diligent to enter that rest, so that no one will fall, through *following* the same example of disobedience. ¹² For the word of God is living and active and sharper than any two-edged sword, and piercing as far as the division of soul and spirit, of both joints and marrow, and able to judge the thoughts and intentions of the heart...."
> HEBREWWS 4: 9-12

Some Christians endeavour to follow the Sabbath as a day of rest, similarly to Jewish observance although without the Jewish particulars. For many, it's an attitude of seeking rest on Sunday – or perhaps Saturday for some denominations. Some will decline shopping on Sundays, that kind of thing. For others, however, the sense of Sabbath is, may I suggest, a deeper understanding of being in Christ Jesus *all the time*.

Let's be honest, Sunday can be a very busy day for many believers and their churches. But it is *how* I live in the day to day – whatever day of the week. Jesus is my Sabbath. He is my rest. Living from Him, having become part of Him, part of the vine. Part of the Body, I allow the life of the Holy Spirit to direct me and operate through me. In this way, I am ceasing from my own works. I am about His agendas and His business. In partnership with the Lord, the yoke is easy.

It may be tempting to 'add' to the life of the Spirit, especially when we are tested; perhaps we have been waiting on a decision for some time; perhaps a situation is developing oh-so-slowly, and our patience is screaming for us to act. These are the times when the discipline of Spirit-led living needs to kick in.

Recently my wife had a work situation which was, in her view, somewhat precarious and as she foreshadowed an upcoming meeting with someone of status, she was concerned that her (quite understandable) anger would interfere with the Lord's solution.

She role played the confrontation multiple times. You have done the same. Boy, her opposite number would know where the both of them stood by the time she had delivered the tirade which was so deserved. The Lord very kindly intervened. He is like that – kind.

My wife had a dream in which she delivered her scathing assessment of the shambles in question; her opposite number reacted with equal, if not fiercer ire, and when she awoke, my wife realised that her approach was not going to bring the fruit needed. So, she took it back the Lord and dealt with her attitude.

The meeting ensued with a very different 'wife' on show. The outcome was more positive that she could ever have hoped for. In fact, decisions were made that usually ran against company policy but were ones that favoured my girl.

Walking in the Spirit is going to be, if it isn't already, a vital, crucial necessity. I believe that walking side by side with the Lord *has* always been of utmost importance but, perhaps, we are realising it more and more in these days.

UNCTION

We need to get acquainted with our 'unction.' The inner, private, sensitive home of the Holy Spirit in your life. Some have described the still, small voice as an umpire. We shouldn't be so far away from the umpire that we have to strain our eyes to see his movements.

I am grateful to two of my current pastors who, from the first time they spent time with me until now (and, to date, they have spent hours and hours of selfless fellowship with my wife and I,) encouraged me to respect and listen to that inner unction.

We are going to have to accept that we are responsible for our decisions – however often we have received advice from others. We have to stand upon our own convictions. We own our decisions.

I remember one time when I was procrastinating on a difficult decision. I was helped (although at the time I'm not sure I acknowledged it as 'help'!) as my patient listener gave me the scenario of someone needing to take a penalty kick in a football match.

I baulked at the decision before me. I suppose I was hoping that someone may make the decision for me. 'No, Steve. It's a penalty. It's your kick. Yes, you might miss *but at least you will have kicked the ball.*'

It's very releasing to accept this responsibility and to know that the Lord understands our struggles. He knows that we want to 'get it right'. He knows that our inner unction is speaking, and it will really help us to listen if we stay in a place of rest. Rest is the soil in which revelation grows.

Our spirit man is already in rest. The Holy Spirit reigns in our spirit. Our soul – our mind and emotions – are probably still catching up to the fact. Remember, they have had years and years of experience in many of our lives; they understand what it is to be independent, to use the natural eyes and ears and mind as sources of wisdom and understanding.

Then we get saved and it's all change. We come alive in the deepest, inner place. *He* takes His place. He makes Himself at home. He is the Spirit of truth. He is truth. He is omniscient, knowing all things, things apparently hidden, and things seen. And He prompts us in His love. He is purposeful and entirely intentional. He has entered our lives on the Father's mission.

The Father's mission is to ensure that we grow into the likeness of Jesus Christ and that the Kingdom of God continues to advance. We will need to be able to stand upon the decisions that we have made. Some decisions are our 'ball' to kick. There is just no getting away from it. We grow, we strengthen, we gain spiritual backbone as we take these decisions on.

Rest allows you to wait; there may be a decision that requires a particularly speedy resolution. Perhaps you genuinely have no choice but to go left or go right. Then, you can only do what could be expected of anyone. You make the best decision that you can, knowing what you know, and sensing where your unction is sitting on the issue at hand. The Lord is our perfect redeemer – He is more than able to overrule if he so chooses.

As we grow in responsibility, there may be decisions to be taken that involve not only ourselves and our families, but wider circles of believers. Some of you will have the widest of spheres of influence. I bless you, in Jesus Name, to live from the rest Who is Jesus, Himself. We are to trust Him and not lean on (rely on) our own understanding.

Reasoning can be very persuasive. Your unction may be showing you differently. If so, I would go with your unction every time.

> "[13] But when he, the Spirit of truth, comes, he will guide you into all the truth. He will not speak on his own; he will speak only what he hears, and he will tell you what is yet to come. [14] He will glorify me because it is from me that he will receive what he will make known to you. [15] All that belongs to the Father is mine. That is why I said the Spirit will receive from me what he will make known to you."
> JOHN 16: 13-15

Our Spirit-led unction will never contradict the word of God and will always glorify Jesus Christ. I love how the verses above reveal God's heart to share Himself and His works with us! Notice the amazing Godhead that have been adopted by – the unity between Father, Son and Holy Spirit is indeed perfect.

"[Jesus] has offered us a new identity – His identity. No longer separated from God, but now united with God. No longer stained by sin, but now clean from sin. No longer slaves, but now free. No longer guilty before God as Judge, but now loved by God as Father"

David Platt

14
WAG THE DOG – WHOSE GLORY?

I have another movie that I would like to share with you.

'Wag the Dog' is certainly a unique story. It serves as a very apt parable on the theme of 'needing to get the credit.'

'Thine Be the Glory!' thunders the chorus of the much-loved hymn. We certainly have little difficulty in our mental assent of the theme, but do our hearts truly resonate to the same degree? May we be secure adults who have understood, to the core of our being, that as ambassadors we are now about the business of the Kingdom and its glory. His glory.

'Wag the Dog' has an all-starring cast, for sure. Dustin Hoffman and Robert de Niro take the stage as partners in orchestrated deception. The US government are suffering in the polls and election day is not far away. They need a boost. They need a sizable swing in their favour if the President is to get his 'four more years'.

They need, they believe, a crisis; one that they can be seen to act decisively on; one that can draw the country's citizens together. They need a cause. *People love to belong to a cause.* Image and perception are going to be everything. The crisis is going to have to be significant enough to grip the heart – maybe the throat – of the nation. And, as a knight on a white horse, the President will be seen to heroically save the day.

Officials (de Niro on a mission) enlist the help of a movie producer, (Hoffman.) Come on, fella. You've produced huge hits on the screen. You've won people's hearts with stunning storylines and visual feasts. What can you do for us?

'How about a war?'
'Excuse me?'

'Yes, a war. Not a *real* war, just a perceived war. A war to utterly distract the public; a war to join hearts, not *against* an immoral president, but *towards* a nation under threat.'

The war's theatre will be – no offence intended to Albanians – a relatively obscure nation as far as the majority of the American populace is concerned. Yes, I've kind of heard of the place but what do I know about it? Nothing, probably.

The plan's success will rest on two issues, mainly. Firstly, the media's coverage will need to be wall-to-wall and consistent in its message. Secondly, those involved in the fabrication must, forever and a day, remain silent on the whole, lurid affair. If this were to get out, the President would surely be in a much worse position than he was in the first place.

The plot moves forward, and the news outlets are jammed with stories of the war; there are fake interviews, AI-produced battle scenes; a famously manipulated scene in which a young actress is filmed (in a studio) clutching a small kitten, the images then superimposed to an apparently war-torn street in a burning, Albanian district. As time passes by, it is decided that this 'war' is going to need a rousing climax to ensure the public's continuing support of the President.

The creative potions are mixed again, and it's decided that a missing hero will fulfil the nation's need to focus on a personable character. He is named Schumann. Wanting to maximise the pathos and patriotism, a song is written to add to the drama of the missing combatant; the public begins to hang old shoes from trees, lamp posts, anything. 'Bring ol' Shoe home!' is the mantra of the masses and, you would think, the President is nearly home and dry.

Realising that it is going to be more than tricky to produce the distant hero, the lies double up again, when it is claimed that poor old 'Shoe' has been killed in action. But no worries. A full, military funeral awaits, and live television is there to capture every sympathetic moment. What a fantastic, consuming, nation-moving affair this whole war has been. Dustin Hoffman is delighted with his success – probably one of his best 'movies' *ever*!

On the day of the funeral, he is watching the coverage on a news channel and his ears begin to burn. Discussing the renewed popularity of the President, credit is given to his campaign team. Yes – it must have been them! Who else could have worked so effectively to swing the voting masses back towards favouring the incumbent leader?

The visiting government-sponsored official visits, remind our increasingly frustrated Hoffman that he is being well rewarded for his 'service', including an ambassadorship and plenty of foreign travel.

'I have to answer to a higher calling,' he counters.

What is happening here? The producer had known the terms of the deal, of the project, since the very start. He had understood the terms but had somehow failed to ingest them. When it came to it – to the reality of others taking credit for his work – he could not abide it. Seeing the exploits so successfully completed, he considers them as the fruit of his 'calling.'

His 'calling' is cinematic excellence. Moreover, he is *to be recognised for it.* He wants the credit. 'That is a complete ...fraud but it looks one hundred percent real!' he protests. He wants to be credited for his unique creation.

The official is expecting his partner in crime to see sense. Surely, any minute he will just calm down and recognise the reality of the circumstances. Surely, he would not – could not – try to blow the whistle on a national military campaign that had captured the attention of the public for many days. Just as it had been designed to do, of course.

As he leaves the room in a temper, the official gives an accompanying security officer a nod. We hear a news flash confirming the producer's sudden and unexpected death from a 'heart attack'.

Kingdom identity recognises that all glory and praise are due to the Lord. When praying before going to the Cross, Jesus asks the Father to make us one, in the Church; Jesus acknowledges that the Father has glorified Him and He asks His Father to glorify the Church through Him, (John 17).

But this is the consequence of the Spirit's work, not our doing or our own efforts to bring praise and honour to ourselves. It is a question that each believer needs to answer honestly, and transparently. Do I want the glory?

Honest answers may waver, and some may also acknowledge the truth; 'Yes, I want some glory. I want some credit. I want to be known. I want others to recognise my achievements.'

Christians are encouraged to testify to what God has done for them. Many church services include a time of sharing such stories. Are we glorifying the Lord or – to be blunt – is our motive really double-sided?

We want to impress others. I love the honest testimony of a man of God that I heard in North America. He was the speaker, one night, at a conference and as he walked through the delegates before the meeting had started, he heard some whispers and references to his name. He loved it. He loved it so much that he decided to walk through the crowd again. Bless him for his honesty.
In recent years there have been initiatives in the world of education to 'protect' children from emotional damage by limiting – or practically eradicating – competition between them. The 'healthy' way forward, apparently, is that 'everyone wins' because everyone is equally important.

Forgive me – this is nonsense. There is nothing wrong with some healthy competition and I believe that winning and losing are part of life and that confronting both of these experiences is all part of building character.

My focus here is on the recognition that our *driver* in life is our desire to allow the Holy Spirit to have His way because He will glorify the Father and the Son. Earthly medals and awards may be enjoyed, but we are to set our hearts elsewhere – on things above, (Colossians 3). Kingdom achievements last. They bless God and His Church.

Kingdom people are about the Kingdom's business.

"No Christian can be a pessimist, for Christianity is a system of radical optimism"

William Inge

15
NOISE

Of course, the aim of the government-strung media, in 'Wag the Dog', is to keep the public satiated.

Satiated, yes. Full. *Distracted.*

The world's noise has a demonic agenda behind it; to keep people from Christ and to keep Christians from intimacy with Christ.

Noise seeks to prise you from the most treasured place – *rest.*

We read it in a previous chapter. Those who know their God shall be strong and will do exploits. These are divine adventures planned for us before the foundation of the world. Heaven is backing us with all of its resources to play our part in them.

What a wonderful call! What a privilege! Our come-close Lord has chosen to involve us in His works. How delightful.

Our lying enemy will do his best to mess with your mind and to convince you that you are not the beloved, chosen son that the Bible declares you to be. In other words, Satan's business is to lie to you about your identity.

He wants to muzzle you, drain you of confidence and cause you to retreat. He wants you to settle into sloth and to lose your edge. He will try to distract you with a million and one other interests, activities and goals.

The enemy surely knows that you won't fall for any obvious 'mega-lies.' Not that a heavy slam-dose of doubt or unbelief is necessarily completely out of the question; much more likely, he will aim at any insecurities in your sense of identity, often reminding you of your past or magnifying your current shortcomings.

He may encourage you to waste your energies on trying to 'make happen' what God has already accomplished, to appeal to your soul rather than relying on the truth that is forever embedded within your spirit.

We have to be solid on the provision and finished work of the Cross. There is no way around this. It is the Cross that *is* our solid, immovable ground. The Cross is our legal document in the heavenly realms where it is known that Jesus Christ is Lord and where it is known that the called-out ones transact Heaven's business based on this blood-bought, grace-provided standing.

Society is going to make some noise.

> "[20] But the chief priests and the elders persuaded the crowds to ask for Barabbas and to put Jesus to death. [21] But the governor [l]said to them, "Which of the two do you want me to release for you?" And they said, "Barabbas." [22] Pilate *said to them, "Then what shall I do with Jesus who is called Christ?" They all *said, "[l]Crucify Him!" [23] And he said, "Why, what evil has He done?" But they kept shouting all the more, saying, "[l]Crucify Him!"
> MATTHEW 27: 20-23

This is no neutral ground. We are operating in enemy territory. You and I may not like it, or want to admit it, but this whole Christian life is very much a spiritual deal and those of us who are in Christ Jesus are marked people.

We are marked on two counts. Firstly, we are marked with the seal of Jesus Christ. His Spirit in us is a deposit, a remembrance, of our divine inheritance. Secondly, the heavenly realms absolutely know who we are and His light in us is evident to watching angels, demons and other heavenly beings.

Looking back at that scene when Jesus was before Pilate, I wonder if you have seen movie portrayals of the proceedings. Even now, having known the Lord for over forty years, I see the Lord Jesus before the Romans, a crowd of baying antagonists behind Him. I still hope that, in some way, voices will speak up for Him, leading to His release. Ridiculous, of course, because it was written that He should pass through that agonising valley and that justice should be absent in the hands of fallen humanity.

And so, the noise! The clamour! The very attempt to suffocate Pilate's thinking. Today, it may be your radio, your TV, your computer, talk shows, radio phone-ins and the like. All of them, almost without fail, bring the same narrative viewpoint. Unbiblical views. Views of tolerance, apparent common sense and people's 'rights.'

Every 'right' under the sun is highlighted and promoted, which has always been the case; these may seem like they are 'modern age' movements but they are not. These disputes have been here since the day dot and always stem from the same pot – the clamour for independence from God.

The latest news story, plot, threat or concern. As much as I find much of the debate and 'revelations' brought by YouTube subscribers fascinating and occasionally informative, I know that my eye and ear gates are to be focused on the activity of Heaven. We need the Holy Spirit to help us to discern truth, falsehood and irrelevance.

Imagine a situation in which you and I were in each other's company, and I was seeking to prevent you from going about your necessary business. I doubt that I would 'blow my cover' by assaulting you or by doing some other ridiculous action. No, I would probably try to distract you by holding you in conversation about a major interest of yours. I would never get the blame, either. It will have been your decision to remain engaged with our interaction rather than press on with what you needed to be doing.

The enemy works exactly like this. Noise. Titillation. Diversion. An invitation to be involved in something of no value.

Do you remember when Jesus' mother and brothers came to see Him?

> "[19] And His mother and brothers came to Him, and they were unable to get to Him because of the crowd. [20] And it was reported to Him, "Your mother and Your brothers are standing outside, wishing to see You." [21] But He answered and said to them, "My mother and My brothers are these who hear the word of God and do it."
> LUKE 8:19-21

Jesus' focus was entirely upon what He saw His Father doing. There are so many miracles and acts that Jesus did that are not recorded in the Bible. The Bible tells us this very thing;

> detail, I suppose that even the world itself *would not contain the books that *would be written.
> JOHN 21:25

Jesus was very active. But He was only busy with His Father's Kingdom business.

Have you been accused (perhaps very gently or subtly) of not 'doing enough' or of not showing enough interest in a cause, a project, or a person? You are not showing the same dedication, apparently, as others.

Actually, it doesn't matter at all what others may think. Your and my only responsibility is to seek to heed the voice of the Holy Spirit. Where He leads, there will be fruit. There will be purpose. There will be Kingdom advance and profit. His peace will overrule in the challenges. Boy, there will be challenges.
We will be confronted in the heavenly realms. We are *worth* confronting because of Christ Jesus within us and because of His mandate in our lives. We will be provoked, discouraged at times, goaded, and even led to an apparent precipice of bewilderment. The Kingdom is advancing and it is advancing against just these kinds of obstacles.

THE PIED PIPER

I remember walking along Green Street in east London towards the Boleyn Ground, home of West Ham United FC.

I have walked that street many times, usually with a quickened pace, eager to reach the hallowed, claret and blue destination. On one occasion, I remember hearing distant music. I couldn't quite make it out but I was conscious of the presence of the Holy Spirit, too. As I continued towards the stadium, I encountered four Christians who were in the middle of an outreach.

Impressive. The location is a rich, ethnic mix although probably Muslim, in the main. It would have taken courage to proclaim the Lord's Name and the team did so with authority. The Lord's presence was evidence that this ground was theirs.

There is a very different noise that seeks to inhibit believers and to mould them towards a mediocre, compromised Christian walk. Rather like the Pied Piper of Hamelin, the enemy would seek to lead us en masse in the direction of a diluted, powerless Christian experience. Our souls – our minds and our emotions – would prefer to avoid confrontation and to seek comfort in agreement and in company.

I believe that many churches seek to work with others with this motivation. Outwardly the steps taken to promote unity may be impressive, but are these endeavours led by the Holy Spirit or is the enemy working to strip church groups from their heaven-sent mandates?

As we follow the leading of the Holy Spirit, we will find ourselves networking and in precious relationships with people whom we may not have expected to be close allies. There will be a quiet, inner assurance as the Lord leads in this way. There is, and will only ever be, one Body of Christ. Worldwide, we are members of the same holy, blood-bought family.

KINGDOM NOISE

The still, small Voice is the most certain, life-giving and affirming voice we will ever know this side of Heaven, when we shall see Him face to face.

To hear Him, to sense Him, to know His nearness; these are truly beautiful aspects of our walk in the Holy Spirit. Such a gentle, loving, abiding Voice – so quiet, in one sense, but surpassing the roar of a lion in intensity and power. His voice is measured; He is always in control, always calm towards us.

Don't be fooled by the interpretations of Jesus' anger in the Temple when He overturned tables and shouted at the businessmen. Such anger is not directed at us. We have become sons, seated on the other side of the Cross.

The noise of the Kingdom has many facets. Primarily, it is the noise of a home. Voices in relationship, trust and intimacy. Laughter, shared humour, joy in the presence of The Presence. Himself.

Then there is the noise of passion. Passion of expression and passion of freedom. Personalities liberated to express themselves as the Maker fashioned them to be. Fearless, no one is shy or embarrassed in Heaven because *we are fully known, fully loved and complete in our belonging.*

Thankfully, we do not have to wait to experience a slice of this reality. "Thy Kingdom come, Thy will be done on earth as it is being done in Heaven." So, we may rest in who we have become in Christ. We may live, now, from that seated position of sonship.

Prayer can be noisy. It doesn't have to be so for it to be authoritative and effective. But, sometimes it is raucous, as it reflects the desires and activity of the Holy Spirit who is at work. There is an inner roar – a fire – a burning – it is God who is authoring and confirming change; the enemy and his influences are being displaced and there is a victory shout.

This is not the soulish clamour of needing to be heard or recognised among or above the throng, this is, rather, the collaborative joining of voices who are in release, of people who 'see' in the Spirit what God is doing. These moments are never planned, truly. They occur as God moves. They are about Him, not us.

When the Holy Spirit came at Pentecost in Acts 2, there was noise.

> "¹When the day of Pentecost [a]had come, they were all together in one place. ² And suddenly there came from heaven a noise like a violent rushing wind, and it filled the whole house where they were sitting. ³ And there appeared to them tongues as of fire [b]distributing themselves, and [c]they [d]rested on each one of them. ⁴ And they were all filled with the Holy Spirit and began to speak with other [e]tongues, as the Spirit was giving them [f]utterance."
>
> ACTS 2: 1-4

Supernatural noise. Noise from Heaven, heard on earth. Amen, let Heaven be seen and heard on earth, Lord Jesus. See the passion of the Holy Spirit! He couldn't wait to be among those guys! A "noise like a violent, rushing wind…" He was about His purpose and that alone.

How we long for the presence of God among us, don't we? *Don't we?* I sincerely hope that we do, for without His presence we may as well just stop what we're doing. Who are we following if He is not leading? Surely there is no one else but Him that we would wish to follow.

We experience the presence of the Lord in many of our church meetings, don't we, and also at home and among friends? Isn't He so often the unseen but very present Other among us?

In Acts 2, He comes in a mighty way. He fills the house, we are told. I think it is a miracle that He manages to contain Himself within that room! Quite how His fiery presence did not spill out through the walls is remarkable.

Actually, it did spill out, right? The disciples, once empowered and speaking in tongues and other languages, left the room to be seen by those who were marvelling outside.

The noise of misunderstanding will manifest around us, too. I hope we are not afraid of being misunderstood. Onlookers joked that the disciples were surely drunk, until they began to reason that it was still morning. As the Lord's presence moves around and through us, religious people may mock and reject what God is doing, just as it happened in Acts.

The Pharisee spirit has always failed the recognise the Lord, even though the Scriptures lie open in front of its face. It will speak out, at times, against His presence and His people. There is an arrogance and pride that resists yielding to the moving of God. It professes allegiance to Him but fails to recognise His company and His hand at work. It prefers the sound of its own voice, its own reasonings, its own limitations. And it will seek to limit others to those same restricting boundaries.

Believers who are secure in their Kingdom identity will recognise the source of noise; the gentle, yet authoritative prompting of the Lord or the driving, pushing agenda-saddled voice of the world?

It is not for us to be intimidated; we are part of a winning Kingdom, but strangers in a world under the thumb of demonic entities. The world's celebrations for Christless agendas ring hollow even though they may be widespread. We know that the firm victory lies with our Saviour and His

Kingdom – and many, hungry souls are thirsty for the reality of His abundant life.

The Church has a voice. A prophetic Church is one that makes some noise – she declares the glory, majesty and love of the Saviour. Our opportunities may seem, sometimes, like a drop in a bucket but every contact, impartation and touch from Heaven *counts*.

Every move we make, inspired and fuelled by the Holy Spirit, contributes to the advancing Church and advancing Kingdom.

"I'm a born-again Christian, but that's not the coat that I wear. It's just how my heart's been changed."

Tony Vincent

16
LIVES OF WORSHIP

The Bible encourages us to consider others as better than ourselves. In that spirit, I am going to assume that most of those who may read these pages understand and live lives of worship to a degree that I have not as yet discovered.

I expect, like me, that you are increasingly seeing that a life of worship is not principally about the period in a church meeting or service when everyone is singing. I am not saying that these times are not part of our worship. I am saying that worship is far, far greater than that.

Jesus has fulfilled the requirements of the Ten Commandments that were written to the Jews. He has fulfilled the entire Torah, the entire Tenakh, the Jewish scriptures. And which two commandments did Jesus agree were the most important?

> "4 But when the Pharisees heard that Jesus had silenced the Sadducees, they gathered themselves together. 35 One of them, [a]a lawyer, asked Him *a question*, testing Him, 36 "Teacher, which is the great commandment in the Law?" 37 And He said to him, "'You shall love the Lord your God with all your heart, and with all your soul, and with all your mind.' 38 This is the great and [b]foremost commandment. 39 The second is like it, 'You shall love your neighbour as yourself.' 40 On these two commandments depend the whole Law and the Prophets."
> MATTHEW 22: 34-40

Jesus is describing a life of worship that spills into loving others. The second is an expression and consequence of the first. As sons and daughters of the House, we have a boundless opportunity each day to love the Lord intentionally and to deepen our friendship with Him. We are then going to love those whom we meet because the Lover of their souls' lives in us.

Our lives can express His *worth* in every capacity. Whether we are in the workplace, in a shopping centre, on the road or in a coffee shop, the Holy Spirit is about the business of revealing Jesus to us and through us.

'Let's have a time of worship now, shall we?' Of course, we know what is meant by that; a time of corporate praise, a time to come together in His anointing. This usually is accompanied by music and songs and hymns, but these accompaniments are *expressions* of the worship we have chosen to lift to Him.

Our intent is key; "You shall love the Lord…" The active, living Holy Spirit in our lives makes this a reality for us. Without Him, we can do nothing, without Him, our songs are just songs. Our flesh cannot bring forth anything of the spirit life.

I remember a meeting many years ago in which the Spirit of God was moving powerfully. A group of young people sat at the back of the room; as God moved, they began to wander towards the front. It was an expression, on their part, of a desire to be involved, to participate, to embrace what God was doing.

An over-enthusiastic observer decided to 'help God out'. He began to encourage the children to get to the front; in so doing, I'm afraid that he interfered with what God was doing by His spirit.
May we let God do it? May we take our hands off. May we be prepared to wait.

God is our lover. Lovers initiate. The Beloved follow their Bridegroom. Everything that God touches becomes something precious and lasting. In days to come, and they are surely right at the door, we will need to know assuredly that it is the Lord who is building and leading our churches. Our own strategies and reasoned efforts are not going to do the job. They will be insufficient to withstand the pressure of the anti-Christ spirit of the world, and will not be suitable carriers of His purposes and provision.

We may manage to look good for a while and may even manage to increase the size of our congregations and church houses. But to what end?
"Unless the Lord builds the house, They labour in vain who build it;"

> "If the Lord does not build the house, it is useless for the builders to work on it." - God's Word Translation
> PSALM 127: 1

If the Lord does not build the house, it is useless for the builders to work on it.

I want to be part of a Church that loves her Saviour, allows the Holy Spirit to have free reign and is one that draws in the hurting lost through the felt, manifest presence of God. That's my *starting* desire. That would be a terrific base to grow from.

Lives of worship. Eyes towards Jesus and His dwelling place, the heavenly realms. Divine order sought in our homes and in our workplaces. Divine order in our relationships. "On earth as it is in Heaven." Authority in the name of Jesus, understood – known – deeply in our hearts from our conscious alignment with His shed blood on the Cross. Born into the family of God, now sons, now friends of the Lord and ambassadors to the world.

God will bless these church bodies and show them not only their own mandate, but also that of other groups of believers; these may be neighbouring churches in a geographical sense, or maybe not. There are no boundaries and no-go zones in the Spirit.

I love it that a small church in the UK may hugely impact a ministry in Botswana, and vice versa.

This is Kingdom Identity. Worship is integral to the Kingdom of Heaven because its King is timelessly and consistently worthy of our adoration, wherever we may be, whoever we may be with.

And our Lover is likely to respond in the most inventive, unexpected ways! In His Presence, anything – anything at all – is possible.

"You must know, rest in, think through, & act upon our new identity - you are in Christ"

Sinclair B. Ferguson

17
LONE RANGERS

There are not supposed to be any lone rangers in the Kingdom of God.

There are going to be particular circumstances whereby a believer, or a small group of believers, are extremely isolated. This may be for an extended time. It may be for a much shorter season.

It will not be because individuals have intentionally decided to 'go it alone.' I have to say that this kind of independent lifestyle is unbiblical and very much to be avoided.

The Body of Christ is just that – a body. A very unique body.

We not only need each other but we have actually become part of one another. Jesus' prayer for us and for those who would continue His ministry immediately after His departure is clear.

> "[18] As You sent Me into the world, I also have sent them into the world. [19] For their sakes I sanctify Myself, that they themselves also may be sanctified in truth. [20] I do not ask on behalf of these alone, but for those also who believe in Me through their word; [21] that they may all be one; even as You, Father, *are* in Me and I in You, that they also may be in Us, so that the world may [a]believe that You sent Me."
> JOHN 17: 18-21

As Jesus prays for his disciples and for those of us who would follow them through the ages, He makes it clear that His heart is for us to be one – to be in unity. Unity requires relationship.

As each of us is born again by the power of the Holy Spirit, we fundamentally have an audience of One – the Lord God. But the immediate consequence of being born again is our adoption into the Father's family.

Whatever our natural, earthly circumstances may be, every Christian has millions of brothers and sisters!

And we need each other. A rounded Christian identity understands the prime importance of the Body of Christ. As Paul describes, whether I am a thumb, calf muscle, eye or freckle in the divine body – I feature! Somewhere!

We are born to connect and once we have been re-connected with our God, we are set to connect with one another; there will be marriages, friendships, small groups, church groups and congregations; there will be conferences, concerts and camps; there will be ministries that will gloriously discover that, beyond the natural eyes of the participants, God has been drawing people together and drawing their hearts to His beating heart.

There have been many, many lone rangers. God will have mightily blessed them, I am sure, to the degree to which they operated according to His leading.

But there has to be accountability.

There would be less falling into sin of all kinds if there was greater accountability amongst the Body of Christ. We each make our choices, and that is true. But we were not designed to go it alone, carry vision entirely on our own or minister in endless meetings with no one else's input.

It makes no sense that the Lord would equip His church with apostles, pastors, prophets, evangelists and teachers if individuals were supposed to operate alone. Some believers can barely handle a night away in a hotel, away from family.

According to an article from Baptist News Global in 2021, 68% of churchgoing men and 50% of pastors regularly watch pornography. This is a fairly calamitous statistic. I heard of one major hotel chain that reported that the adult film channels were used more when Christians were attending their conventions in town, than at other times

It is wonderful that each believer carries an anointing – the very presence of the Lord; but there is also a powerful corporate anointing as the Spirit moves in a church body and among churches.

I suppose there is something very appealing about being the man or woman under the spotlight, on the stage, visible on the platform. For sure, some in the Body of Christ will need to be there from time to time. There are believers who run from the spotlight and others who are more often there.
What is key is what God is doing through that minister's life. To carry the responsibility of ministering to larger groups of people is no small thing; the support of the Body is needed, and also godly oversight.

As a worship leader, I am under authority to my church leaders. Our corporate times of praise are a 'together' thing. This accountability frees me to pursue the Holy Spirit and His direction and to be adventurous! Liberty is being in the light.

I want to stress the sense of adventure and excitement there is in discovering that the Lord is bringing genuine unity within a Church fellowship or perhaps leading groups to work together under the Spirit's leading.

This is a work of God. It is initiated by the Holy Spirit. It is not a repeated refrain of 'Bind Us Together'. The Holy Spirit is building and equipping His Church. What He does, lasts. What He does is precise, effective and efficient. That is the identity of His work and activity.

"The Church needs more people willing to wash feet, not just point out they're dirty or complain that they smell"

Mark Hart

18
HOW MANY CHURCHES?

Kingdom mentality sees that there is *one* Church. The Bible says that the Lord places the lonely in families.

Family is the unit of currency in Kingdom building. It is no surprise that Satan spends relentless energy in seeking to undermine the biblical, family unit. The media is doing its best to portray as many different varieties of family as there are TV channels.

There are some amazing stories out there of gallant, fearless and determined single parents who have loved and sacrificed for their children. I cannot honestly imagine the pressures that they may have faced and the toll that those challenges have taken upon them and their children, too. Their commitment has been laudable and the young adults that many of these parents have raised are testament to mutual respect and devotion.
At the same time, I have no hesitation in standing for the position that God's design is for a man and woman to come together in marriage and for children to be nurtured in that family unit. Girls and boys need a father, and they need a mother, too.

Fathers offer strengths that are particular to them, as do mothers.

A church family will work as a biological family seeks to work; I believe that the Lord plants us in a church unit and that our place there *matters*.

He knows the giftings and calling upon each of our lives and has established and is building church families which will express His heart in many different ways.

But there is one Church and one Head.

> "[12] For even as the body is one and *yet* has many members, and all the members of the body, though they are many, are

> one body, so also is Christ. ⁱ³ For [ᵃ]by one Spirit we were all baptized into one body, whether Jews or Greeks, whether slaves or free, and we were all made to drink of one Spirit."
> 1 CORINTHIANS 12: 12-13

and

> "¹⁶ For [ᵃ]by Him all things were created, *both* in the heavens and on earth, visible and invisible, whether thrones or dominions or rulers or authorities—all things have been created through Him and for Him. ¹⁷ He [ᵇ]is before all things, and in Him all things [ᶜ]hold together. ¹⁸ He is also head of the body, the church; and He is the beginning, the firstborn from the dead, so that He Himself will come to have first place in everything."
> COLOSSIANS 1: 16-18

Have you noticed the father-type figures in your church? And the mothers? I don't mean the literal mothers – although it may well be them – I mean those individuals who, day after day and week after week, support others with these parental elements of character.

I remember in one church, there was a delightful old couple who really were as grandparents to many in the body; they would invite you round for a meal on Sunday, talk about life (theirs and yours), have a wonderful listening ear and then, just before it was time to leave, would pray for you. And I mean, really pray.

Bert went to be with the Lord, first. Flo followed him very soon after. Within a few weeks of their earthly departure, an elderly couple joined from a neighbouring church. You could almost instantly see that the Lord had plugged the 'grandparents' gap with this warm, gentle couple.

We have already discussed the (commonly called) five-fold ministry in an earlier chapter; not every church body will have a whole bunch of evangelists, prophets, or teachers. But I do believe that as the Lord establishes church cells according to His plan and design for them, He will add the necessary ministries to them.

ONE TOWN, ONE CHURCH

In one town, there may be many churches of a range of denominations. I have to say, that the sign on the door is a lot less significant than the signs that the Lord is doing amongst the people.

Perhaps there is a Church of England body or two, or three? A Baptist church? Methodists? Perhaps there are house churches and Pentecostal groups and churches meeting in school halls. Or cinemas.

Perhaps some meet on Sunday and others on Saturday. I know of a church in north London that meets on a Saturday night in a local cinema, as families find it easier to organise themselves then rather than early on a Sunday morning.

There will be Catholic churches and United Reformed. There will be large and small groups. Some will appear to be full of life and others sleepy and in need of life. The sign on the door will often give no clue as to which is which.

The born-again believers in these groups are the Church. And those in the neighbouring town are the Church. All those in the county, the country, the continent and all of the continents together *are the Church of Jesus Christ.*

God is establishing churches because He is building His one, single Church. There is only one. Because there is only one Bride for our Bridegroom.

Each of us and each of our church families are part of this glorious, blood-bought, advancing Body of Christ. Colossians 1: 16 -18 again:

> "16 For [a]by Him all things were created, *both* in the heavens and on earth, visible and invisible, whether thrones or dominions or rulers or authorities—all things have been created through Him and for Him. 17 He [b]is before all things, and in Him all things [c]hold together. 18 He is also head of the body, the church; and He is the beginning, the firstborn from the dead, so that He Himself will come to have first place in everything."
>
> "He is also the head [the life-source and leader] of the body, the church; and He is the beginning, the firstborn from the

dead, so that He Himself will occupy the first place [He will stand supreme and be preeminent] in everything." - Amplified Bible
COLOSSIANS 1: 18

God is looking for Kingdom-minded believers, ministers and leaders. They will not seek to build for themselves but for the Lord. They will be the workers, as in Nehemiah, who will focus on His priorities and have His glory as their priority.

One Church, one Kingdom. The complete reality of this awaits us as described in the final book of the Bible, Revelation.

> "[15] The seventh angel sounded his trumpet, and there were loud voices in heaven, which said: 'The kingdom of the world has become the kingdom of our Lord and of his Messiah, and he will reign forever and ever'."
> REVELATION 8: 15

And

> "[10] Then I heard a loud voice in heaven say: 'Now have come the salvation and the power and the kingdom of our God, and the authority of his Messiah.'"
> REVELATION 9: 10

And

> "[6] Then I heard what sounded like a great multitude, like the roar of rushing waters and like loud peals of thunder, shouting: 'Hallelujah! For our Lord God Almighty reigns. [7] Let us rejoice and be glad and give him glory! For the wedding of the Lamb has come, and his bride has made herself ready. [8] Fine linen, bright and clean, was given her to wear.'"
> REVELATION 19: 6-8

Amazing grace how sweet the sound
That saved a wretch like me
I once was lost, but now I'm found
Was blind, but now I see

'Twas grace that taught my heart to fear
And grace my fears relieved
How precious did that grace appear
The hour I first believed

My chains are gone, I've been set free
My God, my Savior has ransomed me
And like a flood His mercy reigns
Unending love
Amazing grace

The Lord has promised good to me
His word my hope secures
He will my shield and portion be
As long as life endures

The earth shall soon dissolve like snow
The sun forbear to shine
But God, who called me here below
Will be forever mine.

Chris Tomlin, Louie Giglio

19
THE POWER OF THE TONGUE

God speaks. We have been created in His image and so we get to speak, too. Our tongues are designed to be an asset. As Kingdom residents, we can use our tongues to bless with extraordinary power. Unlike anyone who is outside of the realms of Heaven, the Holy Spirit will harness this miracle of muscle to decree *eternal change and transformation.*

When you consider that we have such an opportunity, you appreciate the wonderful privilege that we have, as believers, to bless and proclaim words of life.

The life of the Spirit of God contains power, love and might beyond our current ability to comprehend; nevertheless, we are learning. We desire to learn, as teachable sons and daughters. Our Counsellor is ever so willing to share what He knows.

DESTRUCTION

To exercise authority is one thing; to use our tongues to counter enemy strategies and plans is a beneficial employment of the tongue; to bless, to decree, to prophesy from the heart of the Father are highly valuable, evidently.

However, I would suggest that among the Body of Christ, there are far too many instances of careless, manipulative and even blatantly abusive talk. We are Kingdom people. We all make mistakes and may lose our cool, from time to time. But this kind of oral malpractice is unacceptable.

In May 1985, Bradford City hosted Lincoln City in their final home game of the season. What was hoped to be a day of great celebration for the whole town, due to the Bantam's promotion from Division Three into Two, was to become nothing short of a catastrophic nightmare.

The stand with a wooden roof along the side of the pitch had been officially condemned and was due to be torn down and replaced with a steel structure, at the culmination of the season. There was just one more game to play.

Somebody threw a smouldering cigarette to the floor. They had probably done the same thing many times before. Perhaps they had done so every home game that season. And the season before?

Only this time, this 'throwaway act' was to have devastating consequences. The flickering cigarette end found its way between the wooden planks, which formed the terrace's floor, and fell through to the ground below, ground which had seen a build-up of litter over the previous months, maybe years.
At around 3.40 pm, a small fire became visible and was noted by attending football commentators. This means, of course, that the spark had become a flame some minutes before the sighting.

James speaks of fires in his New Testament letter:

> "[4] Look at the ships also, though they are so great and are driven by strong winds, are still directed by a very small rudder wherever the inclination of the pilot desires. [5] So also the tongue is a small part of the body, and *yet* it boasts of great things. See how great a forest is set aflame by such a small fire! [6] And the tongue is a fire, the *very* world of iniquity; the tongue is set among our members as that which defiles the entire body, and sets on fire the course of *our* [c]life, and is set on fire by [d]hell. [7] For every [e]species of beasts and birds, of reptiles and creatures of the sea, is tamed and has been tamed by the human [f]race. [8] But no one can tame the tongue; *it is* a restless evil *and* full of deadly poison. [9] With it we bless *our* Lord and Father, and with it we curse men, who have been made in the likeness of God; [10] from the same mouth come *both* blessing and cursing. My brethren, these things ought not to be this way."
> JAMES 3: 4-10

I am sure that the analogy is vivid and pretty much self-evident. In less than four minutes, fire engulfed the Bradford stand. Despite many, many heroic acts of bravery which occurred as supporters and staff attempted to free those who were trapped in seats and at turnstiles, a calamity was never going to be averted.

Fifty-six people died that day and over two hundred and fifty more were injured. A carelessly dropped cigarette. A lifestyle of dropping them, probably. A carelessly dropped word. Dropped from a tongue that, as James explains, blesses the Lord in one moment but then delivers death the next through a concoction of 'deadly poison.'

IDENTITY PROCLAIMS

> "⁴³ For there is no good tree which produces bad fruit, nor, [z]on the other hand, a bad tree which produces good fruit. ⁴⁴ For each tree is known by its own fruit. For men do not gather figs from thorns, nor do they pick grapes from a briar bush. ⁴⁵ The good man out of the good [aa]treasure of his heart brings forth what is good; and the evil *man* out of the evil *treasure* brings forth what is evil; for his mouth speaks from [ab]that which fills his heart."
> LUKE 6:45

The Holy Spirit is about His work of sanctifying believers; this will involve a lot of 'undoing' as well as building. Let us come to Him, abide with Him, rest with Him. Let us allow Him to shine His striking but gentle light upon our hearts. I don't want to be dropping any verbal cigarettes, do you?

Jesus continues to teach his listeners in Luke 6 by asking them a question.

> "⁴⁶ "Why do you call Me, 'Lord, Lord,' and do not do what I say?"
> LUKE 6:46

Because, dear Lord, we want to profess that You are Lord with all of our hearts, but, in truth, we may not yet have yielded 'all' of our hearts. There is a mess at the bottom of the terracing. There is latent anger, uncleanness, unforgiveness and hurt. And we have spoken and landed verbal firebombs at others from those broken places.

So, the Father invites His Kingdom children to come to His healing waters and bathe. Be refreshed. Be revived. And where there is unforgiveness on our part, we will have to confront it and bring it to the Cross because there is no other way. There is no more convenient, shortcut.

And as we come to Him to do that, there is a warm embrace and an encouragement to press on into the adventures that He has marked out for us. Perhaps we have been looking back. There is a time to face past hurts and injustices. There is a time to recognise and own our hurts and mistrust of others because of what they have said and done.

But our precious I AM is inviting us to turn our gaze, once more, upon Him. He is our source, our supply, our orchestrator and the finisher of His own work. He is the Lord, He is sovereign and He has never yet missed a beat. This is the stunning God that we belong to, the one who calls us His own.

> "[19] So then you are no longer strangers and aliens, but you are fellow citizens with the [a]saints, and are of God's household, [20] having been built on the foundation of the apostles and prophets, Christ Jesus Himself being the cornerstone, [21] in whom the whole building, being fitted together, is growing into a holy [b]temple in the Lord, [22] in whom you also are being built together into a dwelling of God in the Spirit."
> EPHESIANS 2: 19-22

Citizens, residents, and members of the household which has the Lord Jesus Christ as its foundation. Together, we are the Church, a Body of people who have been rescued, redeemed and appointed to His purpose – that He should be present among His people.

We have an identity to truly treasure. Pinch yourself, every now and again, and remind yourself that it is true!

"God treated Jesus on the cross as if He lived your life so He could treat you as if you lived His."

John MacArthur

20
WINEMAKER

Jesus Christ has never had any issues with his sense of identity. Or, perhaps I am wrong.

Growing up as a child, as gorgeously depicted in the movie, 'The Young Messiah', the boy Jesus is perfectly comfortable with His relationship with His Father, although as the incarnate God made-man, He wrestles with His abilities and the timing of their revelation to the world.

Of course, it's fiction, I get it. Our Bibles don't tell us too much about our Lord's childhood. Nevertheless, there are pointers to Jesus being very aware of the need to walk this human deal out, step by step with His Father. As must we, too.

CANA

Jesus goes to a party. It's a wedding. How apt that His first recorded miracle takes place at a wedding party. We will surely witness an almost indescribably wonderful wedding party of our own when we are fully reconciled with Jesus in the new Heaven.

Song-writer Chris Rice describes a moment when he falls asleep and has a vision from the Lord:

> "Lazy summer afternoon
> Screened in porch and nothin' to do
> I just kicked off my tennis shoes
> Slouchin' in a plastic chair
> Rakin' my fingers through my hair
> I close my eyes and I leave them there
> And I yawn, and sigh, and slowly fade away
> Deep enough to dream in brilliant colours
> I have never seen

> Deep enough to join a billion people
> For a wedding feast
> Deep enough to reach out and touch
> The face of the One who made me
> And oh, the love I feel, and oh the peace
> Do I ever have to wake up …"

As this book draws to a close, I would love to take a further look at the beauty, the timing and the touch of the One that we love and have come home to.

Cana is a salutary reminder that nothing – absolutely nothing – is impossible for our Lord and that He is motivated by a compassion the depths of which we have barely begun to understand.

> "¹On the third day there was a wedding in Cana of Galilee, and the mother of Jesus was there;² and both Jesus and His disciples were invited to the wedding. ³ When the wine ran out, the mother of Jesus *said to Him, "They have no wine." ⁴ And Jesus *said to her, "Woman, [a]what does that have to do with us? My hour has not yet come." ⁵ His mother *said to the servants, "Whatever He says to you, do it." ⁶ Now there were six stone waterpots set there for the Jewish custom of purification, containing [b]twenty or thirty gallons each. ⁷ Jesus *said to them, "Fill the waterpots with water." So they filled them up to the brim. ⁸ And He *said to them, "Draw *some* out now and take it to the [c]headwaiter." So they took it *to him.* ⁹ When the headwaiter tasted the water which had become wine, and did not know where it came from (but the servants who had drawn the water knew), the headwaiter *called the bridegroom, ¹⁰ and *said to him, "Every man serves the good wine first, and when *the people* have [d]drunk freely, *then he serves* the poorer *wine; but* you have kept the good wine until now." ¹¹ This beginning of *His* [e]signs Jesus did in Cana of Galilee, and manifested His glory, and His disciples believed in Him."

Yes, it's the familiar 'water into wine' account, but let us go deeper. Cana means 'place of reeds' in Hebrew. This matters.

Cana's meaning describes God's design for the place. The Hebrews built with reeds – you could make an entire house from them but, more often than not, reeds were used for the roof of the dwelling.

Jesus was about to show Cana and its residents that everyday building would not make the grade in the supernatural Kingdom of God. The Kingdom is built through and for supernatural, divine purpose. And Kingdom people operate in the same realm.

The wedding took place on the third day. Good things happen on 'third' days. Life happens. 'God life' is revealed and dull, earthly authorities have to make room. It's a joyful occasion; I wonder if you can picture it. You may have seen depictions of the event in a movie or television series.

Jesus loves a wedding. Weddings were His idea! Father, Son and Holy Spirit love the joining of a man and woman who will become one flesh – who will taste at least something of the supreme intimacy of the Godhead.

There is a whole bunch of people there, Jesus's family, for a start. The gang. Now that might be challenging, don't you think? You are about to launch a ministry that will be known all over the world for time immemorial – and the 'fam' is present.

Mary shows compassion. 'Darling son, they have no wine. They're going to be embarrassed. People are going to know that they have miscalculated. It's the big, big day and this is going to mar the celebrations.'

As Christians, we identify with Jesus Christ. Our identity is embraced in Him. Despite questioning Mary's concern, He is going to do it anyway. He is going to act.

Can I encourage you, please? Jesus is ready to act on your behalf. You are loved and you are worth it. You are worth His love, His attention and His gaze and, having paid the ultimate price for you, He is dedicated to you *in covenant.*

There are six water pots. The number six speaks of the efforts of man, in the Bible. These pots have been used many times, probably, in Jewish purification rituals. They have been filled and re-filled with water but, as yet, *not a single person has found inner cleansing* through their use.

Something is about to change. Now, the multi-gallon pots are in the hands of the Potter.

TOUCH

Jesus has decided what He is going to do with them. That is enough. His decision *is* His touch. He doesn't appear to physically touch the pots, at all. 'Draw *some* out now and take it to the [s]headwaiter.'

One of the blessings of the New American Standard Bible is the notation of words that were added by the translators to ease a common, modern reading. But see how the verse above gains significance when we realise that Jesus did not ask the servants to pour water from the pots. He didn't actually state what He knew the water had become. The servants only had to 'draw' and Almighty God had done the rest.

The touch of God brings a new, divine flow of a unique substance. *This particular wine has never before been created or tasted.* Your, and my life, are as the wedding wine of Cana. We are unique and we have been concocted for a special season.

Note that it was the bridegroom's responsibility to provide the guests with wine. Jesus, our Bridegroom takes the responsibility beautifully.

NEW IDENTITY

In our passage from John 2, Jesus does not address Mary as his mother but calls her 'woman.' He is separating Himself from His earthly, natural relationship and identity and fully adopting His spiritual, Heaven-sent calling. He is not going to be held back by anyone. He only answers to His Father and does what He sees His Father doing.

Water is not going to do the job. We need wine. We need the Blood of Jesus, represented by wine at the Last Supper, as our foundation and bedrock. Christ Jesus, Himself, is our cornerstone. What He builds, lasts. What He establishes, He feeds, nourishes and prospers. Our lives are about His glory, His fame, His renown.

The wedding is honoured. Jesus has blessed the occasion not only with His presence but with a demonstration of His heart and of His power. Exactly the things that the world needs to see today.

The best wine. The only wine that could taste like *that*. Jesus has turned the tables, and not for the last time! The timing is His and not the world's. He is our eternal God and He is unbound by any of our expectations or customs. Kingdom living requires nothing less than the finger of God. We, His Body, get to participate and honour His Name as we are directed by the Holy Spirit. That is a Kingdom people who know their raison d'etre.

'Every man serves the good wine first,' we read. But His wine is a constant vintage. A forever vintage and forever magnificent. The precious Blood of Jesus will always fuel His Kingdom wonderfully. In Heaven, there is no decay. Nothing rots, nothing spoils, nothing diminishes in value or quality.

The end of the passage we have been considering tells us that this event saw a manifestation of Jesus' glory. May the very same be our desire, too. May our energies go into that. For as His glory was seen, the disciples 'believed'.

Scripture tells us that a man can only receive what He is given from Heaven. So Jesus must be seen; seen in us. With words and without them. May the next person we meet experience this, as Heidi Baker of Iris Ministries has long encouraged us. And then the next one.

We only know in part; who is already a saint? Who is a potential saint? We don't really need to know, except that if we love the one in front of us, we will play our part well. May He say to each of us:

> "You did well. You are a good servant who can be trusted." -
> International Children's Bible
> MATTHEW 25:23

Sons and daughters who know who they are and have become intimately acquainted with the beautiful, incomparable Son of God will bear fruit. Grafted into the divine vine, fruit will grow as a consequence of exposure to Kingdom living. Living from our given position in heavenly places.

On earth, as it is in Heaven.

"When we allow people in our lives to define us or when we make up our own definition of who we are, we will be veering away from the Truth. The only One able to give us our identity is our Maker."

Sunshyne Gray

POSTSCRIPT
LITTLE OLD LADY

My lovely mum is in her later eighties. She loves Jesus and has a beautifully simple friendship with Him. She talks to Him. He tells her things – such as how to clean the lounge curtains. Real life.

Mum sometimes describes herself as a little old lady. I don't see her that way. She is my mum. She was always only five feet and one and a half inches tall at her 'height'. She is now considerably less. But she is active, walks every day with a lively, toy poodle called Tammy, and endeavours to encourage at least one person every day.

Mum is courageous. We lost Dad three years ago and it has not been easy, especially for Mum. Jesus always saw people from a heavenly viewpoint. He was prepared to ignore his own mother and brothers if it meant focusing on what He saw His Father doing.

> "46 While He was still speaking to the crowds, behold, His mother and brothers were standing outside, seeking to speak to Him. 47 Someone said to Him, "Behold, Your mother and Your brothers are standing outside seeking to speak to You."[ao] 48 But [ap]Jesus answered the one who was telling Him and said, "Who is My mother and who are My brothers?" 49 And stretching out His hand toward His disciples, He said, "Behold My mother and My brothers! 50 For whoever does the will of My Father who is in heaven, he is My brother and sister and mother."
> MATTHEW 12: 46-50

The earthly order is temporary, but the heavenly order is eternal. It is very easy to see each other's flaws and failures, but we need to consider one another with the honour and prestige that Heaven accords us. We are no longer lost sinners, but sons and daughters of the House of the Father.

Mum is a vibrant, Holy Spirit-empowered woman. I know that Father thinks she is amazing. Her childhood wasn't easy. She was a child of the war, which she experienced at very close hand. She grew up through displacements and some unkindness, although she always seems to focus on aspects to be grateful for.

She persevered through trials and married my dad. The couple had two sons, Simon, the elder, and me, the younger.

PIECE OF PAPER

When my brother and I were young boys, Mum would visit some of the elderly in the local area; she would offer to do their shopping, completely voluntarily.

One particular old soul lived alone just around the corner from our road. She lived in absolute squalor.

I got to see this first-hand. There were a few occasions when I substituted for Mum. I was quite happy to pop round to these homes and be given a short shopping list and a small sum of money to cover the price of the groceries.

You may be invited in, you may not. On at least two occasions, I was invited in to this particular house while the little old lady fetched her purse. Oh.My. Goodness. The living room was an absolute mess. Utterly filthy, it appeared not to have been cleaned for – well – months? Years?

I imagine that today, with the increased media focus on the well-being of 'old folks,' that support would be offered in such an appalling scenario. I remember the smell, the grey and black of the room. I remember the disorder. And I remember her offering me 50p, I think, for my trouble.

Mum continued to visit this lady; she did so several times more. And then one day, there was no answer when Mum knocked at the door. I think you know what is coming. The discovery of the little old lady's death was obviously a shock for Mum. But that wasn't the half of it.

As the police and other authorities began to sift through the piles of rubbish and debris that littered the house, they found wads of bank notes stuffed in various places. It would appear that the elderly resident had possessed the means to live a rather different lifestyle, but that – somehow – the opportunities had passed her by.

An even more shocking discovery was that of a framed certificate that sat on a bedroom wall. Closer examination revealed this document to be a money order worth a huge sum of money. Tragically, the lady had not understood what it was. She had effectively filed something that was worth many hundreds of pounds, funds that would have set her up very usefully in her latter years.

That piece of paper contained enormous potential. It was never realised. May that not be the case with the promises pertaining to our lives.

We were adopted into the family – let us live in the House. We have become sons and daughters – let us grow in love for the Father. Our old nature was crucified and disempowered at the Cross – let us believe and walk in the identity that is ours in Jesus Christ; forgiven, redeemed, appointed, and mandated to represent the Kingdom of God.

"At the heart of what it means to be a Christian is to receive a new identity. In Jesus, we do not lose our true selves, but we become our true selves, only in Him"

John Piper

NOTES

Introduction:
https://www.brainyquote.com/topics/identity-quotes   Tim Tebow quote

Chapter 1:
https://www.goodreads.com Henri Nouwen quote

Chapter 2:
https://www.brainyquote.com   Lecrae quote

Chapter 3:
Freedom Beyond Comprehension by Joan Hunter (Whitaker House 2012)
Sermonindex.net   T Austin-Sparks quote
speeches.byu.edu   Russell Nelson quote

Chapter 4:
The Silent Seduction of Self-Talk by Shelly Beach (Moody Publishers 2009)
https://www.brainyquote.com Dan Quayle quote

Chapter 5:
The Power of a New Identity by Dan Sneed (Sovereign World Ltd 2012)
https://www.azquotes.com/quote/849525   Timothy Keller quote

Chapter 6:
https://www.austin-sparks.net By T Austin-Sparks
https://www.brainyquote.com Bear Grylis quote

Chapter 7:
https://gracequotes.org/topic/identity-christ_in/ Randy Smith quote

Chapter 8:
https://www.austin-sparks.net/english/004620.html

Chapter 9:
https://www.azquotes.com Timothy Keller quote

Chapter 10:
https://www.azquotes.com   Timothy Keller quote

Chapter 12
Quote – www.theoverflowing.com

Chapter 13
https://gracequotes.org   David Platt quote

Chapter 14
https://www.brainyquote.com   William Inge quote

Chapter 15:
https://www.brainyquote.com   Tony Vincent quote

Chapter 16:
https://www.azquotes.com   Sinclair B Ferguson quote

Chapter 17:
https://baptistnews.com/article/the-ongoing-epidemic-of-pornography-in-the-church/
https:// www.azquotes.com Mark Hart quote

Chapter 19
https://gracequotes.org   John MacArthur quote

Chapter 20:
https://sunshynegray.com   Sunshyne Gray quote

Postscript:
https://gracequotes.org   John Piper qu

ABOUT THE AUTHOR

Steve Hawkins, a British writer, has authored several titles including *'From Legal to Regal'*, *'Blood and Glory: The Cross is Still the Crux'*, *'The Pointing Finger'* and *'When God Laughs'*.

He has a passion to see Christians discover the freedom and delight of the Gospel of Jesus Christ, much motivated by his own struggles with legalism in earlier years of his faith walk.

Steve has led prophetic worship for many years and enjoys his involvement with prophetic teaching and ministry.

Having previously worked in financial services, catering and adult learning, he now teaches in a secondary school in Hertfordshire.

Steve and his wife, Stella, are part of the New Zion Christian Fellowship in Welwyn Garden City, UK.

CONTACT THE AUTHOR

Speaking / ministry events
Steve can be contacted at purplejeans09@gmail.com

www.ingramcontent.com/pod-product-compliance
Lightning Source LLC
Chambersburg PA
CBHW041141110526
44590CB00027B/4092